THE PSYCHOLOGY
OF INVESTING

Other books in the *Wiley Investment* series

Cyber-Investing: Cracking Wall Street with Your PC, Second Edition
David L. Brown and Kassandra Bentley

The Investor's Anthology: Original Ideas from the Industry's Greatest Minds
Charles Ellis with James R. Vertin

Mutual Funds on the Net: Making Money Online
Paul B. Farrell

It Was a Very Good Year: Extraordinary Moments in Stock Market History
Martin S. Fridson

Independently Wealthy: How to Build Wealth in the New Economic Era
Robert Goodman

The Conservative Investor's Guide to Trading Options
LeRoy Gross

The Psychology of Investing
Lawrence E. Lifson and Richard A. Geist

Merton Miller on Derivatives
Merton Miller

REITs: Building Your Profits with Real Estate Investment Trusts
John Mullaney

The Art of Short Selling
Kathryn F. Staley

The Stock Market, Seventh Edition
Richard J. Teweles and Edward S. Bradley

Market Magic: Riding the Greatest Bull Market of the Century
Louise Yamada

THE PSYCHOLOGY OF INVESTING

LAWRENCE E. LIFSON

RICHARD A. GEIST

John Wiley & Sons, Inc.

New York • Chichester • Weinheim • Brisbane • Singapore • Toronto

This book is dedicated with love and affection to our wives,
Marcie G. Lifson and Susan Schiff Geist,
and to our children,
Deborah and Jennifer Lifson
and
David, Mark, Daniel, and Sarah Geist

This book is printed on acid-free paper. ∞

Copyright © 1999 by Lawrence E. Lifson and Richard A. Geist. All rights reserved.

Published by John Wiley & Sons, Inc.
Published simultaneously in Canada.

No part of this publication may be reproduced, stored in a retrieval system, or transmitted in any form or by any means, electronic, mechanical, photocopying, recording, scanning, or otherwise, except as permitted under Section 107 or 108 of the 1976 United States Copyright Act, without either the prior written permission of the Publisher or authorization through payment of the appropriate per-copy fee to the Copyright Clearance Center, 222 Rosewood Drive, Danvers, MA 01923, (978) 750-8400, fax (978) 750-4744. Requests to the Publisher for permission should be addressed to the Permissions Department, John Wiley & Sons, Inc., 605 Third Avenue, New York, NY 10158-0012, (212) 850-6011, fax (212) 850-6008, E-Mail: PERMREQ@WILEY.COM.

This publication is designed to provide accurate and authoritative information in regard to the subject matter covered. It is sold with the understanding that the publisher is not engaged in rendering professional services. If professional advice or other expert assistance is required, the services of a competent professional person should be sought.

Library of Congress Cataloging-in-Publication Data:

ISBN 0-471-18339-3

Printed in the United States of America.

10 9 8 7 6 5 4 3 2 1

PREFACE

It is now a well-known fact that between 1970 and 1990, 75 percent of professional money managers underperformed the Standard & Poor's 500.* More informal data also suggests that large numbers of individual investors lose money in the market even when investing in those mutual funds that outperform. The obvious question that emerges from these statements is: Why do so many bright, competent, and creative investors and money managers fail to outperform the market? There have been many answers to this question. On the professional side, it has been argued that transaction costs lower managers' performance; the competition is so fierce that it obviates a winner; the market is so efficient that stock prices reflect all available information and prices adjust too quickly to this information to allow a competitive edge; institutions are nothing more than a surrogate for the market and therefore cannot outperform themselves. On the individual investor side, we know that investors buy too high and sell too low, buy on rumors and hot tips, believe too many gurus, are not disciplined enough, lack a consistent approach to the market, and frequently misjudge management of their companies or mutual funds. What almost every experienced investor will admit, however, is that endemic to these ostensibly rational explanations are deeper psychological forces that seem to underlie most of the costly errors on Wall Street and Main Street.

With an increasing number of baby boomers turning to the stock market to secure their long-term financial survival, it became increasingly clear to some of us at Harvard Medical School Department of Psychiatry that we needed to further explore how both group dynamics and individual personal psychology affect investor's decisions. Two of our Harvard Medical School faculty (Drs. Richard Geist and John Schott) had the distinction of being both practicing psychotherapists

---

*C. Ellis, *Investment Policy* (Homewood, IL: Irwin, 1993).

and psychoanalysts as well as investment professionals. Both of them published national investment newsletters that not only recommended stocks and mutual funds, but also informed the readership of the psychological factors that influence investing. One of us (Dr. Lawrence Lifson) is Director of Continuing Education at Massachusetts Mental Health Center, a major teaching hospital of Harvard Medical School. He conceived the idea of creating an annual conference on the Psychology of Investing that would bring together a faculty of seminal educators and leaders in the fields of investing and psychology in order to explore the interface between human emotions and financial decision making. The objectives of these conferences would include: applying psychology theory to an understanding of money management and investment decision making; understanding the impact of group or "mob" psychology on market fluctuations and investment choices; understanding the psychological underpinnings of contrarian investment theory; exploring the psychological overtones to momentum theory; delineating the psychological dynamics of risk; and understanding expert error and its relationship to financial analysis. The conferences would also elaborate on how both group dynamics and the individual's personal psychology affect investor decisions.

The chapters in this book were selected from presentations delivered at the annual conferences on the Psychology of Investing. When we began these conferences in 1995, psychology, with a few notable exceptions, played a minor role in both practitioners' and academics' thinking about the investment process. Academic research was based on the assumption that markets were efficient and that investors were totally rational decision makers. Even on the practitioner level, it was often assumed by investment firms that investors' psyches had little to do with their performance.

For decades the idea of rationality was like some enchanting siren insidiously summoning us into a world of promised stock market truth. Through the efforts of several groups—behavioral economists, cognitive psychologists, psychoanalytic practitioners, and money managers—all of whom understand that individuals functioning under conditions of risk do not behave rationally, the introduction of psychology into the investment field has now become an increasingly popular and important subject. These groups have all brought new truths and invaluable contributions to the investment world—and probably not too soon because an increasing number of individuals are now depending on the stock market to fund retirement and college tuition.

As Loren Eiseley once pointed out, the discovery of other truths often destroys the reality of the one truth under whose influence a field has long been functioning. We are now beginning to understand more about the interaction of emotions and financial decision making, about the impact of psychology on group behavior, about the many emotional meanings of money, about the ways emotions impact economic analysis, and about the impact of investment firm psychology on money manager performance. Nevertheless, the field remains in its embryonic stages; much research is waiting to be done; much is still unknown about what goes on in the minds of individual investors and groups as they confront the pressures and rewards of committing money to investments with often unpredictable futures.

We hope that this book will generate new hypotheses, create new dialogues, and lead to new truths that will help us better understand the unique characteristics of financial markets. To that end we have roamed far and wide in these chapters, including thoughts, ideas, and questions that challenge traditional ways of thinking. Some of these insights may prove to be a stepping stone to significant changes in how we think about the investment process; others may fall by the wayside. Only through such incipient dialogue, however, will we be able to build a body of knowledge that can greatly improve how human emotions affect financial decision making.

LAWRENCE E. LIFSON
RICHARD A. GEIST

Newton, Massachusetts
January 1999

CONTRIBUTORS

David Dreman, M.B.A. Chairman, Chief Investment Officer, and Founder of Dreman Value Management, L.P.; author: *Psychology of the Stock Market: Contrarian Investment Strategy; The Psychology of Stock Market Success;* and *The New Contrarian Investment Strategy;* columnist, *Forbes Magazine.*

Donald L. Cassidy Senior Research Analyst, Lipper Analytical Services; author, *It's When You Sell That Counts* and *Plugging into Utilities.*

Louis K. C. Chan Department of Finance, College of Commerce & Business, Administrator, University of Illinois at Urbana-Champain.

Basil Chapman Editor, *The Chapman Marketline and Trendswatch,* Newton, MA.

Richard A. Geist, Ed.D. Instructor in Psychology in the Department of Psychiatry, Harvard Medical School; founding member and faculty, Massachusetts Institute of Psychoanalysis; President of The Institute of Psychology and Investing.

Steven Halpern Editor/Publisher, *Dick Davis Digest* and *Income Digest;* syndicated columnist, Knight Ridder Newspapers; author, *The Road to Stock Market Success.*

Samuel L. Hayes, III, D.B.A., M.B.A. Jacob H. Schiff Professor of Investment Banking, Harvard Business School; coauthor or editor of six books.

Mark Hulbert Editor, *The Hulbert Financial Digest;* author, *The Hulbert Guide to Financial Newsletters;* columnist, *Forbes Magazine;* Editorial Board, American Association of Individual Investors.

Narasimhan Jegadeesh Department of Finance, College of Commerce & Business, Administrator, University of Illinois at Urbana-Champain.

Josef Lakonishok, Ph.D. William G. Karnes Professor of Finance, University of Illinois; author, *The Incredible January Effect: The Stock Market's Unsolved Mystery.*

Harry Levinson, Ph.D. Clinical Professor of Psychology Emeritus, Department of Psychiatry, Harvard Medical School; chairman, The Levinson Institute; author: *Men, Management, and Mental Health; Organizational Diagnosis; The Great Jackass Fallacy; Ready, Fire, Aim;* and *Psychological Man.*

John Schott, M.D. Clinical Instructor on Psychiatry, Harvard Medical School; chairman, Department of Psychiatry, Metro West Medical Center; portfolio manager, Steinberg Global Asset Management; publisher, *The Schott Letter.*

Matthew M. Stichnoth Publisher and editor, *The Wall Street Companion.*

CONTENTS

CHAPTER 1

Investor Overreaction

David Dreman

Contrarian strategies have been around for a very long time, and recently their popularity has been increasing. These strategies are ways of beating the market that are value oriented, using ratios such as: price/earnings (P/E), price-to-book-value, price-to-cash-flow, and price-to-dividends. Investors were slow in accepting contrarian strategies, particularly in the 1960s to 1980s heyday of the efficient market theorists.

Our research shows that all contrarian strategies do better than the market over time. Using a sample of the 1,500 largest stocks on the Compustat tape, most of which are companies well over $1 billion, the first contrarian strategy was investing in companies with a low P/E ratio. The results for $10,000, if originally invested in 1970, were significantly better than the market. In 1997, at the end of 27 years, the $10,000 would have been $909,000. The same $10,000 invested in companies with low price-to-book ratios and low price-to-cash-flow ratios would have been similar at $850,000 and $712,000, respectively. Even a low price-to-dividends ratio, which would not be expected to do as well, would have done significantly better than the market: $545,000 versus $326,000 for the market. So all of these contrarian strategies worked successfully over long periods of time. The reasons are intimately related to psychology and the way people look at earnings estimates when they make their initial investment decisions and the way they react to them afterward.

Not only do these contrarian strategies work well, research shows they do relatively better in a down market. During the down quarters between 1970 and 1997, the market was down an average of $7^1/_2$ percent, whereas price-to-dividend was down by a little under 4 percent and the other indicators were down within a percentage point of each other at about 6 percent. These contrarian strategies not only do better in a bull market, they provide better protection in a bad market.

The major reasons are behavioral. One of the cornerstones of all finance is the belief of most people on Wall Street that earnings estimates can be precisely fine-tuned. People in general are confident of their estimates. Trial lawyers, for example, on both sides of a case will estimate they have a better than 50 percent chance of winning.

The same kind of research has been done with physicians and psychologists, looking at their confidence in their estimates as against the actual accuracy. A confidence rate of 80 or 90 percent usually results in an actual diagnosis being accurate about 60 percent of the time. The more complex the information processing and the larger the amount of information to be integrated, the more complex the decision making gets to be. For the security analyst, there are hundreds, if not thousands, of factors to look at when valuing a company—its related industry and its related international markets, among other factors. To compound the complexity, these are not static factors. All the data are changing at the same time, so the evaluation is an enormously complex task. Analysts are supposed to be good configural reasoners, which means that they are supposed to be able to take all of the disparate and changing information, put it together, and come out with an answer. At least that's what the theory demands of analysts as practitioners. But that is like saying that every chess player will be as good as Kasparov, when in reality only one in maybe 100,000 reaches Grand Master level. Yet the market assumes that all analysts can take in the huge amount of information, process it accurately, and come to the same conclusions.

2

Estimates are exceedingly difficult to make, though the market demands fine-tuned, precise estimates. Research on the efficacy of analysts' estimates shows the average analyst error over a period of 25 years between 1973 and 1997 is 44 percent, annualized.

As practitioners we demand the ability to fine-tune our estimates within 2 to 3 percent. But because the actual average error is 44 percent, if I was estimating a dollar, I would be likely to end up with roughly either $0.56 or $1.44.

Analysts today have far more information available to them as a result of the enormous information technology revolution that has occurred since the 1970s. But they also have all of the other analysts' estimated reports online instantaneously. An analyst for Goldman Sachs knows in a matter of minutes if an analyst from First Boston or Morgan Stanley changes his or her estimate and knows the reasons why. Despite the volume of information and the improved online reporting from companies, the analyst error rates are getting higher over time. Even though there's a demand for precision, it has not happened.

Remembering that analysts and Wall Street demand fine-tuned forecasts, assume I'm buying an Internet stock and paying 100 times revenues for it. I want to make sure that I know the company is actually going to earn $5 a couple of years out. Because I pay a high price, I have to be very precise. But what my research shows is that analyst estimates are not precise. In any quarter, only 30 percent of estimates fall within the desired plus-or-minus 5 percent range. In other words, 70 percent of those 100,000 consensus estimates are outside the desired and expected range. Even plus-or-minus 10 percent is an enormous difference, and 48 percent of analyst estimates can hit that range. Only 55 percent of analysts' estimates can get within plus-or-minus 15 percent.

In our research we looked at whether the imprecision was industry specific because some industries are more volatile than other industries. It was suggested that bad estimates or high estimates really only occurred in the very volatile industries. But we found that, if anything, the estimate errors occur right across the board. The average estimate error in each industry was 50 percent, and the median error was 43 percent. The estimate errors are extremely high over time.

There are a number of reasons why estimate errors might be too high. One is that they are not only high but also optimistic. Analysts over the last few decades have been too optimistic on estimates. So not only is there error, but there is this second factor–optimism–that one major study showed was in error by almost 9 percent a year.

Again, if I buy an Internet stock and I need a dead-on estimate, the chances are that I'm going to have an estimate that's going to be overoptimistic, and that is going to hurt me over time. One of the behavioral questions to ask here is why these estimates are not changed. Analysts know that there are major reactions to their estimates when they're off, and people know that analysts' estimates have been plagued by major errors for almost 50 years. Yet analysts continue to practice as they always have. Analysts looking at a company's quarter to make an estimate will not look at a broad band such as $1 to $1.50 in order that they might catch an error. Rather, they will look at a small band of performance, say $1.13 or $1.15. So it's a single forecast, and the probability of making a correct forecast from these figures is very small.

The next thing that we want to look at very briefly is what happens when there are major errors. First of all, analysts and the institutional investors and individual investors who use analyst estimates are confident that these estimates will work well for them over time. Our research shows that there is a very consistent pattern when analyst forecasts miss the mark.

What we find is that there are really two types of errors with analyst estimates: surprises that are "event triggers" and surprises that are "reinforcing events." Stock prices react very differently to the different types of surprises, and surprises have different impacts for popular stocks versus unpopular stocks. If a stock is popular and there's a negative surprise, the perceptions of that stock change. We call it an *event trigger*, but another term could just as easily be a *perceptual change*. The change doesn't happen all at once. I will use Internet examples because I think that's an area that at some point is going to be an enormous debacle. That area is going to crash and will probably result in one of the worst downturns in the postwar period, accompanied by a lot of the other aggressive growth stocks. If we get disappointments and we paid a lot of money for the disappointing stocks, the surprises are what we would call *negative event triggers.* They trigger us to change our outlook about the companies, to scale down expectations. Conversely, an event trigger for a company that is out of favor—for example, a bank stock in the 1990s when banks were in crisis—would be a positive event trigger or surprise. People think the worst of these unpopular stocks, but if they surprise positively, the market looks at these stocks, and perceptions change. They are stocks that investors no longer look at as negative. So the positive surprise will have more of an effect on the stocks' performance.

The other kind of surprise is what we call the *reinforcing event.* If a stock is popular and it has even better earnings than expected, the positive surprise will affect perceptions only minimally. A good stock should have good earnings. And conversely, if a stock that's out of favor has earnings that are a little worse than expected, the negative surprise doesn't hurt the stock much.

So there are two very distinct types of surprises that we see in the stock market, the event triggers and the reinforcing events. Compaq Computer, for example, experienced an event trigger in 1996. It was an out-of-favor company that had better-than-expected earnings early in 1996. The stock went up by about 30 percent. An example of a reinforcing event is Duracell in 1995. It was a well-liked company with earnings ahead of market, but the positive surprise didn't help its performance all that much. People just expected a company like Duracell to have good earnings.

Our research studied the overall effect of surprise on popular stocks and unpopular stocks, again using a sample of about 1,500 companies. What it showed was that all surprises, positive and negative, are very favorable for unpopular stocks. In the quarter studied, they outperformed the market by better than 1.4 percent, and for the full year, the unpopular stocks still outperformed the market by 4 percent. Whatever the market does, they seem to do 4 percent better. Conversely, favored stocks are not helped by surprises. Surprises hurt stocks that are in favor.

If those surprises are broken up, it's interesting to see how the news affects stocks differently. Over the quarter, positive surprises for all unpopular stocks resulted in unpopular stocks outperforming the market by $3^1/2$ percent, and the effect gets stronger for the full year— 8.1 percent better than the market. So positive surprises have an enormous effect on the unpopular stocks, because people look at them again and think that the unpopular stocks are not as bad as they had previously assessed them to be. Positive surprises for popular stocks have a much lower effect in the quarter, and the surprise effect declines for favored stocks during the full year. So positive surprises work very much in favor of stocks that are contrarian stocks that people don't like, and they work against stocks that are in favor.

The impact of negative surprises is also very different for popular and unpopular stocks. What we see is that the unpopular stocks that experience a negative surprise in the quarter are down 0.8 percent annualized, and by the end of the year of the surprise, they shrug off the surprise, underperforming by a mere 0.4 percent. Negative surprises for stocks for which we have high expectations are murderous. They are down almost 4.5 percent in the quarter and are down over 9 percent after the full year. That's 9 percent under the market. So there's an enormous difference between how surprise affects favored and unfavored stocks.

For an event trigger, or perceptual change—a positive surprise for an unpopular stock or a negative surprise for a favored stock—our research shows that overall there's something like an 8 percent or higher difference in spread in the quarter. And after one year, the impact is more than 17 percent. The other classification of surprises— reinforcing events—is the case in which people expect good stocks to have positive surprises or bad stocks to have negative ones. These surprises don't impact prices that much. Overall the impact is a little under 2.5 percent in the quarter. By the end of the year, there is almost no impact at all. The differing impact clearly demonstrates the two different types of surprises: Event triggers have significant effects on stocks, whereas reinforcing events have little effect in the long run.

An event trigger or negative surprise on a high-flying stock knocks the stock down very sharply. A positive surprise for contrarian stocks will push the stocks up. People look at them, and in both cases they reevaluate. In the second case, the stocks are just too cheap, and the positive news results in more positive appraisal.

When we look at the effects of surprise, not for one quarter or for one year but for five years, what we see is that there's an enormous impact in the first quarter that carries all the way through, so that an unpopular stock with a positive surprise consistently outperforms the market for 20 quarters. And the return is something like 35 percent above the market. Conversely, the negative surprise on the favored stock causes it to underperform in an asymmetrical way to the positively surprised out-of-favor stock. It underperforms consistently for 20 quarters, so that there's an enormous difference in the return because of the surprise.

We then considered whether the number of earnings surprises made the difference between the impact of event triggers and the impact of reinforcing events. What we saw was that the numbers aren't very different. The number of positive surprises is actually higher for the favored stocks, and there is statistically no difference in the number of negative surprises. So overall, the number of surprises didn't affect these results.

Lastly, we looked at whether it was the size of the surprises that caused the differing impact. Again we saw that the size of the negative surprises was pretty similar for the lowest P/E (unpopular) stocks and the highest P/E (popular) stocks. The sizes of the positive surprises were actually a little bit higher for the highest P/E group. So the size of the surprises did not account for the different impact.

I believe there have to be behavioral explanations then that cause the consistent performance. We have reviewed studies from the 1960s, 1970s, and 1980s, through to 1997, and what is fascinating is that there's a predictability and consistency in investment behavior decade after decade. We found that the best stocks consistently underperform after an earnings surprise and that the worst stocks consistently outperform. This systematic and predictable behavior seems to be explainable by investor psychology.

One of the things that happens is that people tend to extrapolate the past into the future. Extrapolation is a very simple economic concept but an enormously complex psychological one. In the extrapolation many complex psychological forces interact. In cognitive psychology, an important force is representativeness. Recency and saliency of events are major influences on investment decisions. If I see a high-flyer (an Internet stock, for example) that I like and I watch it go up, it makes me forget the long-term probabilities that these stocks don't work. People forget that new issues have underperformed the market over time. The market had a return of 12 percent, far ahead of the 3 percent return of initial public offerings (IPOs) over the 20 years ending in 1990.

People forget. Not only are analysts overoptimistic in their forecasts, but experts are overoptimistic overall. Investors believe that zillions of people will participate in the Internet, even though these stocks have not made any money to date and likely will not for some years.

Overall these Internet stocks have a market value today of $15 billion or $20 billion dollars. Yet what many of them will do is sell advertising, and now they have roughly 20 times the market value of all the public advertising companies in all the world. So we're really in an astounding type of mania, possibly the greatest since the tulip craze.

Something that psychologists certainly know and economists never look at is that people don't learn from their own past mistakes. Economics assumes that we learn, and because we are able to learn, we can correct. Cognitive psychologists have done a number of studies that show that people just don't learn from the past. Because we're not able to learn from the past, we may look at a specific past mistake and decide if we were only more careful we could have prevented it. But we don't. We will still get into a mania almost the same way the next time and the time after. That is why we've had four hot IPO markets since the 1960s.

The Dutch had their tulip bulbs only once, and that was back in the seventeenth century. And the English had the South Sea bubble. But we've had recurrences of these new-issue manias four times in 30 years, and this one is the biggest of all. Over $150 billion of new issues have been issued to date. It, too, will likely end in a debacle because we can't learn. New issues might be the psychotic part of the market, if you will, whereas the big stocks—the overvaluation of what we think are the best stocks and the undervaluation of what we think are the worst—are the neurotic part of the market. But by using the contrarian strategies I outlined at the beginning and by staying consistently with them, there is still plenty of opportunity to make money over time.

CHAPTER 2

The Emotions of Risk

Richard A. Geist

Every investment in the stock market involves making decisions the outcome of which is unknowable and unpredictable. This fact has fostered discussions of risk that are centered around the concept of *uncertainty*, which the investment community has translated to mean volatility of potential returns as an objectively measured statistic. Thanks to Modern Portfolio Theory, a voluminous literature now exists on such objective measures and definitions of risk and on the most effective methods for managing them. Risk as a subjectively experienced emotional state, however, has received much less attention, despite the fact that most investors acknowledge that how they respond psychologically to making decisions under conditions of uncertainty can have a dramatic influence on their performance.

As Loren Eiseley once said, "There is a difference in our human outlook, depending on whether we have been born upon level plains, where one step reasonably leads to another, or whether, by contrast, we have spent out lives amidst glacial crevasses and precipitous descents. In the case of the mountaineer, one step does not always lead rationally to another, save by a desperate leap over a chasm or by an even more hesitant tiptoeing across precarious snow bridges."[1]

---

[1] L. Eiseley, *The Unexpected Universe* (New York: Harcourt, Brace & World, 1969), p. 73.

These differing landscapes of the mind create contrasting lenses through which to view the world. One reminds us that the world is rational and predictable based on historical patterns. The other reminds us that however scientific our understanding and ordering of events, there is always a deeply rooted unexpectedness and a not-quite-ordered universe lurking behind our ostensible consistency. Nowhere is this contrast more apparent than in the attempt to define *investment risk*–that slippery topic whose parameters encompass both objective measurement and gut-wrenching emotion. My task here is to delineate the subjective aspects of risk, to discuss the emotional factors that influence one's capacity for taking risks, and to examine some of the ways successful investors perceive the concept of risk.

DEFINITIONS OF RISK

The most widely accepted measure of risk within the investment community is volatility of returns. Academicians assess volatility in several ways: standard deviation measures volatility in absolute terms, that is, how much a portfolio varies from its own arithmetic-mean returns; beta and $R2$ measure volatility in relative terms, that is, how much change one should expect in a stock price relative to the change in a major market index. Betas are then used to measure the ostensible risk of portfolios. For example, if Company X's stock or your portfolio consistently drops (or rises) 20 percent more than the market, it becomes by definition a riskier investment. As there is no free lunch on Wall Street, a corollary to this definition states that the higher the risk, the higher should be the potential returns.

Because of the equating of risk with volatility, some investors place great faith in the idea of risk-adjusted performance, a concept developed by Nobel-prize-winning economist William Sharpe. He argued that it doesn't make any sense to look only at how much money a portfolio made; one must also look at how much risk one took to achieve the gain. Essentially, risk-adjusted performance penalizes volatility, no matter how successful the eventual outcome of the investment.

Some investment professionals have suggested that the risk/volatility equation is too limiting and that a broader risk paradigm is needed. For example, Robert Jeffrey suggested that risk is a function not only of volatility, but also of one's present and future liabilities[2]—in other words the amount of cash one needs to meet future obligations. Taking into account both the asset and the liability sides of the equation and the holding period certainly enhances understanding of risk, but it still fails to deal with the fact that investors (like all human beings) do not always think rationally when making decisions under conditions of uncertainty. This simple psychological fact means that risk, by definition, contains important subjective elements not typically considered or evaluated by the investment community.

Risk can be defined subjectively as the emotional reaction to one's idiosyncratic perception of the chance, probability, fear, amount, or consequence of loss. From an emotional perspective, risk (the psychological reaction to potential loss) is often equated with uncertainty because all investments in instruments that trade in the capital markets involve decisions about an unpredictable future. Investment results are uncertain because they are contingent on the relatively unpredictable performance of a company and its management, the behavior of others in the marketplace, the randomness of events occurring in the world, and the psychological reactions of the investor to each of these phenomena. Uncertainty generates anxiety, a diffuse state of tension that frequently elicits either the illusion of excessive danger or the denial of a danger that should be feared.

Objective risk exists as a mathematical reality. And a variety of well-known techniques can be employed to lower the "chance" of loss: dollar cost averaging, hedging, low expenses, minimum turnover, diversification, careful asset allocation, buying with a margin of safety, sell disciplines, careful fundamental evaluation, and valuation of companies. However much an investor chooses to emphasize and lower objective risk, he or she must still deal with the subjective reality of

---

[2]Robert Jeffrey, "A New Paradigm for Risk," *Journal of Portfolio Management* 11:1 (1984).

emotional responses to risk. Peter Bernstein once commented, "the determining question in structuring a portfolio is the consequence of loss; this is far more important than the chance of loss." The distinction arises frequently in conversations about risk. Tune into your local business radio talk show. Investor A calls up and says, "I don't know whether to invest my money in aggressive funds or to be more conservative." And the talk show host replies, "It all depends on your capacity to tolerate risk. How risk averse do you want to be?" The caller says, "I want to take some risk, but I don't want to lose anything." Investors can tolerate thinking about the chance of loss more rationally than they can tolerate thinking about the consequences of loss.

It is the psychological impact of "consequence" of loss on rational decision making that makes most attempts to categorize investments according to an objective, schematic risk profile so misguided. However much we may acknowledge that there is some objective knowledge of risk that can be known by the investment community and transmitted to individuals, for the majority of investors *risk is a subjective concept intimately related to loss and found not in the external worlds of stocks and bonds, but in the internal and subjective world of the investor.* Concepts such as volatility become relevant in this context only to the extent that they create anxiety that causes investors to sell out at precisely the wrong time. For the return on investment can never be knowable previous to an investment decision, and even after the results are in, an investor still cannot judge how risky the investment actually was.

THE PSYCHOLOGICAL CAPACITY
FOR ASSUMING RISK

The investment literature delineates two major risks for market participants. First is systematic risk, that risk than an investor cannot avoid when participating in the stock market—in other words, those factors, such as interest rates, inflation, and credit crunches, that are endemic to being in the market. If, for example, there is a recession, company earnings and revenues trend downward, changing the psychological expectations of investors and encouraging a lower perceived valuation of fair stock prices. Systematic risk is, by definition, market risk. Second is unsystematic or company risk, which is that risk above and beyond the risk of the market as a whole. It refers to the vagaries of specific management, products, services, industry, and business decisions and how these idiosyncratically affect individual securities in a portfolio. Corporate risk will also be affected by the choice of capital structure (debt versus equity financing) and the life stage of the company (start-up, emerging growth, and so on). The ultimate danger is that an individual company will go out of business.

Company risk can be theoretically and mathematically diversified away by owning 10 to 15 stocks in different industries. Although as Peter Bernstein has correctly pointed out, diversification does not guarantee against loss, only against losing everything at once. Market risk, on the other hand, cannot be eliminated and remains the price one pays for investment rewards. It is important to understand systematic and unsystematic risk, but each remains an external factor unrelated to an investor's subjective perception of risk. Such external factors have never seemed terribly useful in helping to answer the question: "How much and what kind of risk am I prepared to take when investing in the stock market?"

The answer to this question derives in part from factual data: age, income, savings, future need for cash, and investing time horizon. But these answers are more related to capital loss—whether one will have cash to pay necessary expenses in the future. From talking with and interviewing many investors over the years, I have increasingly come to believe that equally important are questions related to the psychological aspects of risk.

GRANDIOSITY

Fear and *greed* are the watchwords of the Street, but there is an overlooked concept that is much more important to the psychological understanding of risk: *grandiosity*, defined as "a strong belief in one's greatness, abilities, knowledge, or character." Its ideational content is most often expressed by both children and adults (and in myths) through dreams and fantasies of flying.

Within the investment world, variations of flying fantasies can contribute to major monetary losses as well as contributing significantly to investment achievements. Fantasies of making an investment so successful that the results will change one's lifestyle is an example of an investment flying fantasy. The extent to which investors diversify versus placing all of their eggs in one basket depends in part on the nature of grandiosity and the degree to which it is integrated into investors' rational and realistic motives. The myth of Daedalus serves to highlight the difference between the grandiosity that carries investors spinning out of control and the more controlled grandiosity that helps investors to achieve their ambitions and ideals.

Daedalus had built a labyrinth for Minos, king of Crete, and upon its completion wished to return to his home in Greece. But he was so useful as an engineer and inventor that Minos refused to let him go. Daedalus and his son Icarus were compelled to stay in Crete against their will. Not being able to leave the island by sea, because the king kept strict watch on all vessels, Daedalus turned to the air. "Minos may control the land and sea," he said, "but not the regions of the air. I will try that way." So he fabricated wings for himself and his young son Icarus out of feathers and wax and gave the whole gentle curvature a shape like the wings of a bird. When father and son were prepared for the escape, Daedalus warned Icarus: "keep at a moderate height, for if you fly too low the damp will clog your wings, and if too high the heat will melt them."

As the two took flight, ploughmen and shepherds on the ground watched them, astonished at the sight, and concluded that if they were flying, the pair must be gods. Suddenly Icarus, exulting in his new-found ability to fly, soared upward toward the heavens. The proximity of the sun softened the wax holding his feathered wings together, and Icarus plunged helplessly into the sea. Daedalus arrived safely in Sicily, where he built a temple to Apollo and hung up his wings as an offering to the god.

A basic psychological truth is given metaphorical life in this mythical story about the assumption of risk and its different fate in the lives of two individuals. On the one hand we learn how painful can be the consequences of uncontrolled grandiosity; on the other hand we learn how real success and achievement may result when such grandiosity is employed in the service of rational ambitions and ideals.

When investors are hot—when they make several investment choices that perform exceedingly well—there is a rekindling of primitive grandiosity. They feel like the basketball player whose every shot floats gracefully through the net in the first half of a game. Invincible, brilliant, and master stock pickers, such investors can do no wrong, make no mistakes. Risk, they believe, is for the faint of heart. They make such insightful decisions that they need not consider the idea of risk.

The brilliant investor feels analogous to the child or the adolescent whose grandiose fantasies confer a sense of invulnerability. There is thus a particular kind of risk—an accident proneness or an error proneness—common to brilliant investors that tends to account for a regression to the mean in long-term performance. In fact, from consultation with many investment professionals, I estimate that the lifetime error rate in professional analysts and money managers tends to be about 40 percent, and the error rate is probably considerably higher—50 to 60 percent—in the general investor population. Only in those few investors such as Warren Buffett, who have their grandiosity well contained, can outstanding performance be maintained.

SHAME AND HUMILIATION

Investing is a performance game, watched closely by the investor him- or herself as well as by others. Investors all need to have their sense of self (which includes judgments about investing) watched, validated, and confirmed. Just as the ploughmen and shepherds gazed intently at Icarus and Daedalus and assumed they were gods, investors–particularly professional investors–live in a fish bowl where their every move is scrutinized. Money managers operate in a public arena dominated by those with myopic time horizons. Quarterly performance records are often public; managers' performances are followed by clients, competitors, and employers; and their capacity to beat the market is judged continuously.

Such public scrutiny predisposes investors to feelings of shame in two areas. First, because most investors are talented, creative individuals who have confidence in their ability to perform well, investor mistakes often leave an individual in a position analogous to a lecturer who tells a joke in front of a large audience and receives a deaf-ening silence. In other words, the investor frequently holds him- or herself up for validation and is left exposed to the vagaries of negative and humiliating responses. Second, because active money managers and individual investors truly believe they can beat the market, they are frequently exposed to a failure in their own internal goals and aspirations. As Andrew Morrison has pointed out, "The nameless mortification and dejection inherent in failing to achieve one's ambitions and ideals is captured by the world shame. For shame is the hallmark of a failure of one's self as it aspires to be."[3]

The sense of being exposed for making mistakes in the market is a thorn in the side of every investor. Those who are able to be humble and realize that three or four stock picks out of ten will do poorly usually attain better rates of return than those who fear admitting mistakes. The fear of public or private humiliation drives investors to dissemble their failures; as a result they never learn from their mistakes. Those individuals who can acknowledge failure

---

[3]Andrew Morrison, "Shame and the Psychology of the Self," in *Kohut's Legacy* by P. Stepansky and A. Goldberg (Hillsdale, NJ: Analytic Press, 1984).

are able to take more risks because they rarely make the same mistake twice.

ANXIETY

Because uncertainty is endemic to the investment process, anxiety (conscious or unconscious) appears to accompany each investment decision. Anxiety manifests itself in multiple ways: it may appear as irritability, shifts in tone or posture, difficulties in communicating, or physical manifestations such as tremor, a lump in one's throat, or a sinking abdominal feeling. Subjectively, when the self feels vulnerable, anxiety interferes with what is called secondary process thinking—the logical, ordered, rational means of problem solving. What one then experiences is a slight regression toward primary process thinking, a form of thinking in which the connection between words and thoughts is based primarily on emotions rather than logic. Thus, if I ask you to give your first association to the word *red* or the word *mother*, and you are in a primary process mode, your associations are likely to be very different than the dictionary definitions of these words. Primary process thinking is closely associated with imagination and dreamlike states in which there are few boundaries or rational sequences.

Investors whose primary process mode of thinking has been demobilized are much more vulnerable to magical thinking—believing rumors, tips, and innuendo. Especially if there are few real facts available to explain a potentially significant company event or lower stock price, one is much more prone to apply fantasy to ambiguous stimuli and to believe the most recent information received. Combining anxiety with a dearth of real information leads investors to apply their internal fantasies to an external phenomenon and then to become absolutely convinced of its "truth." This phenomenon is rampant on the Internet and is relied on by stock manipulators when channeling their inaccurate rumors of fraud and company failure through the media. Its use has convinced many well-meaning investors to panic—a form of group anxiety—and to sell shares prematurely.

THE EXPERIENCE OF TIME

Time is both an objective and a subjective phenomenon. Objectively *time* can be defined as the duration of seconds, minutes, hours, days, months, years, and so on, that can be clocked and measured according to some agreed-upon standards. Everyone knows that a week consists of seven days. However, if you tell your two-year-old that you'll be gone for a week, he or she will have no conception of the length of your absence. Once you leave, your child may experience the week as forever. This brings us to the subjective nature of time. Depending on development stage and emotional state, people all experience time differently. Vacations pass quickly; the workday drags interminably; time occasionally stands still; time passes more slowly for children than for adults. The relationship between everyday clock time (objective) and time as an agent of our psychological life (subjective time) dramatically influences investor behavior; but to my knowledge, it is a subject left virtually untouched by both investors and psychologists.

Subjective time can be defined as the distortions of clock time inherent in each person's psychic life. A familiar scenario will explicate this idea: I recommended a stock that you didn't buy, but the share price tripled in 18 months. You now think to yourself, "Why didn't I buy XYZ at $13? How often will I get a chance to triple my money in so short a time?" On the other hand, I recommended a stock and suggested that the stock could triple in 18 months. You think to yourself, "That's a long time to tie up my money if nothing happens down the road." Why do we experience 18 months as unbearably long when we are about to commit money to an investment while the same period is incredibly short when we could have successfully committed money in the past?

Feelings from the past as well as hopes and fears about the future are continuously active and alive in the present. Investors function emotionally much of the time as if they were living in the present without realizing how past and future fears and hopes unwittingly influence their time perspective. In this way human emotions frequently move contrary to economic interests by interfering with long-term investing.

My own qualitative research suggests that those individuals who experience time as passing quickly have more capacity to tolerate volatility than those who experience time as passing slowly. Two years of waiting for an undervalued stock to finally begin its ascent is more tolerable when units of time pass rapidly. Those who experience time as moving slowly often panic when the market drops 100 points because the psychological perception is one of "in the doldrums forever."

Todd, who experienced time as moving slowly, bought Facelifters (FACE) in November 1993 at $5.13 per share. The stock moved very little for a few months and then went to the $7 range where, with the exception of a few temporary upward and downward moves, it remained for nearly one and one-half years. Todd became bored and unexcited about the stock, despite the company's obvious and continuous increase in revenues and earnings. In September 1995, Todd finally sold his shares in FACE at just under $7. During October the stock price quickly increased to $10.25, and in June 1996, it closed at $28 per share.

Todd explained his decision to sell. "I was getting impatient waiting. There were too many other good opportunities out there that could give me a quick 25 percent gain. I know I should have held on, but I felt like I was in that Beckett play *Waiting for Godot.* Nothing was happening." For Todd, waiting for FACE to move became impossible. Time moved very slowly for him. Passively sitting with the stock seemed much less productive than actively pursuing other opportunities. As with so many investors for whom time passes slowly, a 25% gain per year feels much better than a 400 percent gain during the third year.

For Todd the feeling of not knowing how long he needed to wait for FACE to begin to move left him feeling out of control. He lost his healthy sense of omnipotence about his investment decision, and the resulting anxiety was handled by selling the stock. Investors with a shaky feeling of continuity and control are much more frightened sitting long term with a stock that is not moving.

LOSS

Because risk is intimately connected to loss, particularly the consequences of loss, how an individual has experienced and adapted to loss throughout life becomes a prominent factor in one's approach to risk. All human beings experience both real loss of valued people and emotional losses. If one has not resolved former real or emotional losses, there is a tendency toward blindly eliminating losing situations in the face of downside volatility. This is one reason many analysts downgrade stocks after they have already tanked and why investors often sell at the bottom. They experience an almost paniclike psychological urge to divest themselves of the psychological and paper position of loss without first understanding whether the fundamentals warrant such actions. Such mistakes frequently occur on anniversaries of former losses.

Common to those who have not resolved emotional or real losses is a terrifying feeling when a fundamentally sound stock begins a sharp retreat. As one investor described it, "I saw the stock going down and down and down some more. All I could think of was that I was losing everything. It brought back all the losses in my life. It got to the point where I couldn't stand it anymore and just sold out for a huge loss. I knew I shouldn't be selling, but I just couldn't stand living with that feeling of loss. The monetary loss was awful, but it was such a relief to not think about losing that for a moment it almost made it worth it." Reflecting on one's real or emotional losses and integrating that knowledge into one's investing style not only alleviates much unnecessary panic but also prevents significant denial of loss when the market is volatile on the upside. Avoiding important investment decisions on the anniversary of losses also helps to avoid irrational mistakes.

THE NEED TO BE PART OF THE HERD

As chroniclers of evolutionary biology have pointed out,[4] if one looks carefully at the evolution of the human species, one discovers a time when living and functioning in herds was in the best interest of survival—not only of the individual but of the group (relatives and offspring). Given this history, I believe that the deeply ingrained psychological tendency to function in herds, especially under conditions of risk, was in evolutionary time an adaptive, protective mechanism that remains a built-in part of the human psyche. It is partially responsible for the individual's need to borrow strength, knowledge, and power from looked-up-to others and to feel secure in the sustaining presence of like others. Not only is this tendency elicited when people face perceived threats; it also is readily evoked when they perceive large groups forming around them, and it underscores the reason that contrarian thinking is so difficult to practice. This is a particularly useful piece of information because it helps in understanding why investing does not come naturally to so many people. To invest successfully means that investors must go against a long and powerful evolutionary history of psychological adaptation, which has not selected them for the task.

Particularly when an individual has failed to take in those functions that foster the development of a cohesive self, he or she has a tendency to tune into and fit into the internal state of others. And within this collusive bond, compliance fosters the subordination of

---

[4]D. Kriegman and M. Slavin, "On the Resistance to Self-Psychology: Clues From Evolutionary Biology," in *Progress in Self-Psychology* by A. Goldberg, vol. 6 (Hillsdale, NK: Analytic Press, 1990).

the self to the subservient position of being an extension of another. From an evolutionary perspective this emphasis on respecting authority over researched content and belief had adaptive value for the survival of the group. Within the investment community, there are often high rewards for actions based on imitation rather than independent thinking. But such compliance generally leads to conformity and average performance over the long run.

IMPLICATIONS OF CHANGING DEFINITIONS

If we change the definition of risk to encompass not only volatility as an external property of the market, but also certain properties of the self, then we begin to ask different and novel sorts of questions: Do I experience time as passing slowly or quickly? Do I have any unresolved real or emotional losses? What is my tolerance for sudden change? What is my propensity for shame? Can I tolerate uncertainty without undue anxiety and denial? Do I have more faith in my own judgment than in others? When we view risk as an important internal element that structures our subjective way of interpreting external reality, many of the traditional investment concepts that are taken for granted on Wall Street begin to change.

Example 1: Speculation and Bull Markets

What drives a bull market is not so much greed as grandiosity. When prices continue to escalate, investors being to feel like Icarus—they feel increasingly excited and capable of flying higher and higher. So long as these beliefs are harnessed to a larger rational plan that joins correct data to a grandiose project, these flying fantasies will fuel realistic ambition, for the narcissistic enhancement that comes from this coupling leads to normal psychological buoyancy and pride. Where grandiosity is split off from normal reasoning, however, increasing deficits in investment reality testing will be seen. In the case of greed, the inherent compulsion to make up for deprivation always contains a lack of reality testing and eventually contributes to the investor's downfall.

Currently I see investors at large (the public) in a very powerful attempt to connect their flying fantasies with reality, through increasing attempts to gain a financial education (for example, never before in this culture have we had such a demand for investment clubs and business-talk-radio stations). Thus I believe that those investors who are putting money into mutual funds with the market at these heights are not in a grandiose speculative frenzy; rather they are employing their grandiosity realistically. I also do not believe that a correction will bring an automatic panic in this more rational group for they are unlikely to experience risk as volatility.

In contradistinction, I think that the truly greedy minority will eventually come to grief in the IPO (initial public offering) market and in highly speculative individual stocks. Those whose greed is fueled by archaic grandiosity tend to be continual losers in the market, while appearing outwardly as extremely successful.

Example 2: Small-Cap Investing Is Risky

Small-cap investing has always been considered risky because small-cap prices demonstrate more volatility than large-cap prices. Viewing small caps from other than a price perspective, however, leads to several additional considerations. Small caps tend to be less subject to groupthink than their larger brethren. Institutions shy away from smaller stocks because they literally have too much money to invest. As a result most institutional analysts don't conduct extensive research on small companies, thus we see more pricing inefficiencies. Management of small companies are generally available to talk with investors and supply needed information. Does any of this imply higher risk? Not in the usual sense. What is true about small companies is that they place different psychological demands on investors. For example, the small-cap investor is left alone to distinguish fact from fiction. Functioning in a virtual vacuum, one's grandiose fantasies need only the slight stimulus of a friendly "can't lose" tip to vitiate all remnants of rational decision making. Thus the small-cap investor must constantly guard against rumors, tips, and fantasies that are stimulated by working in a more-isolated environment. Small caps demand enormous time and energy, and when one doesn't devote time and energy to the situation, there is a tendency to create one's own ostensibly rational assessment of a company based on fantasies woven out of a mixture of incomplete facts and wishes that lend false credence to hopes for a 20-point rise in the stock price. With the advent of the Internet, there is also more of a push toward herd mentality; rumors on the Net become facts that motivate irrational investment decisions. It also takes time for small caps to become large caps, and therefore small-cap investing requires unusual patience to reap the benefits of the enormous upside potential of some of these companies. Volatility, however, encourages immediate sales on temporary bad news and immediate profits on temporary good news. This unanalyzed impatience becomes an insidious psychological danger for the small-cap investor. Does all of this mean small caps are more risky than large caps? I think the answer ultimately depends on how one's emotions shape one's internal risk profile, not on the external reality of increased volatility.

SUCCESSFUL INVESTORS

Let me close by offering some observations on how *successful investors* handle psychological risk. Rather than viewing risk as either chance or consequence of loss, they seem to experience it as decoupled from the concept of loss. Decisions become turning points for better or worse, part of the multiplicity of choices that comprise our everyday life's decisions. They are closer to John Maynard Keynes' 1921 statement that "most of our decisions to do something positive can only be taken as a result of animal spirits . . . and not as the outcome of a weighted average of quantitative benefits multiplied by qualitative probabilities."[5]

Such successful investors possess several psychological characteristics that allow this different view of risk:

First, these investors know they will make mistakes, but the mistakes do not threaten their sense of self. They have just as much confidence following a mistake as at the time of the original investment. They do not berate themselves or blame others for mistakes. They reverse directions quickly, understand where they went wrong, and tend not to make the same mistake again. Their self-esteem remains intact despite the loss of money. In fact, most of them enjoy the *process* of making money more than they do the money itself.

Second, the intellectual challenge for these investors seems to replace the concerns with loss. Every decision becomes a challenge to assess not only the correct time to buy, but also the quality of management or the products and services being offered by a company. Investing choices become more than decisions; they have the feel of the ideal tennis shot or the perfect gymnastic move. Investors seem to subscribe to Freud's idea that "The voice of the intellect is a soft one, but it does not rest till it has gained a hearing. Finally, after a countless succession of rebuffs, it succeeds." It is this confidence in their own intellect that allows successful investors to hold on to an imperturbable optimism. Such intense belief in their intellectual capacities allows for failure while turning decision making into an art that is enjoyed for its own sake.

Third, part of what allows a focus on decision making rather than on loss is the investors' capacity to remain slightly aloof from market fluctuations. There is a particular kind of psychological denial employed when they study the media headlines, markets, and stock prices, with a concurrent overriding belief in their ability to correctly assess the intrinsic value of a company and the quality of its management (for example, "So what if the market dropped 100 points. My com-

---

[5]John Maynard Keynes, *A Treatise on Probability* (London: Macmillan, 1921).

pany is still worth what it was yesterday"). The capacity for the right amount of denial is key—too much denial prevents an accurate assessment of reality; too little leads to undue anxieties about loss.

Fourth, nearly all of the investors who have the capacity to decouple the idea of loss from risk seem to establish very strong bonds with another person (or people) while they are engaged in their creative investing. Furthermore, they rely (often unconsciously) on the existence of this bond for the exercise of their skills and talents. We know that such relationships exist frequently in the life of creative writers and artists, but their occurrence in the investment world has been overlooked. According to Roger Lowenstein in his book *Buffett, The Making of an American Capitalist,*[6] Warren Buffett and Charlie Munger seem to have this sort of relationship ("The two of them had a peculiar symbiosis and, as in a good marriage, an aura of inevitability"). And it is clear from Lowenstein's book that Buffett for many years was dependent on his wife's background presence to pursue his work. It appears to me that creative work under conditions of risk often demands such bonds to support one's sense of self.

Finally, investors who decouple risk from loss appear to think of themselves as outsiders. They do not experience themselves as adapted for this world, and they have a history going back to childhood of remembering being different from the others in the groups to which they belonged. These investors were not loners—they had friends—but they experienced themselves as not quite fitting in. Thoreau's notion of walking to a different drummer is applicable here, but with the addition of coming to terms with having taken the road less traveled so that remaining an outsider has become part of an identity that is prized for that particular characteristic.

---

[6](New York: Random House, 1995).

CHAPTER 3

Why It Is So
Difficult to Sell

Donald L. Cassidy

I am not formally trained in psychology and so hesitate to attempt to express or to explain all my observations in technical terms. The approach herein will be to report what I have observed in investors–mainly individuals rather than Wall Street professionals–and thereby allow those who have the requisite medical and psychological training to form the appropriate constructs around these observations.

It would be useful to begin by indicating how, as an investment analyst employed in the equity research department of a regional retail brokerage firm, I came to write my book on selling.[1] One morning during what brokers refer to as the "squawk box talk," I recommended selling a particular stock that I was covering and spelled out my fundamental reasons: the facts regarding the stock had changed; the thesis was no longer valid; so it was time to move on. Afterward, a broker phoned and asked me to detail my reasons because she had a client who owned the stock. But he had bought it several months later and many dollars higher than my original buy recommendation. Now, for him, the stock was down a few points. The broker agreed that my

---

[1]Donald L. Cassidy, *It's When You* Sell *That Counts!* (New York: McGraw-Hill, 1997).

reasoning seemed solid but said she'd never be able to get her client to sell. "He refuses to accept losses and has threatened to fire me if I bother him with bad news," she explained. We then looked at his account to discover some other potential sales, at profits, so there would be no net loss to irk him. The two such candidates, however, had larger profits, so those sales would result in a net taxable gain for the year. "Oh, no," she said, "he hates paying taxes, so he'll refuse to take those profits." Sensing we faced a hopeless situation, I joked that he would never sell a stock unchanged either because it would not yet have done anything for him. Here was a successful business executive, unable to sell stocks regardless of whether they were down, up, or unchanged—a true, although unintending, long-term investor. The certificates could have been framed for hanging because he would never part with them.

Reviewing that conversation, I became convinced that there was an endemic problem here, one worth further investigation. So as I worked with brokers and listened to them and their clients, I made mental notes about selling problems and decided this was indeed a rich lode. Research revealed that more than 20 years had passed since anyone had written on the neglected subject of selling stocks. And having thought and observed and listened and spoken on the topic for the past decade, I am now convinced that no amount of facts or of logical advice will fully enable all investors to conquer the problems surrounding selling because they are deeply psychological in nature.

Clearly, the difficulties investors face involve both external influences and internal drives and motives. With buy-and-hold so well ingrained, even thinking seriously about selling is viewed as somewhat heretical. Currently, investors' ability to deal competently with selling stocks suffers inordinately due to the nearly constant and certainly long-imprinted experiences of a 16-year bull market that has taken the Dow Jones Industrial Average up more than 10-fold. On average, most investors feel that selling is simply the wrong thing to do based on the odds most recently observed. But this cyclical bull market and that misperception created by unusually consistent reinforcement will pass in time, still leaving investors with many unresolved essential issues surrounding selling.

Some of those issues will continue to be systemic external factors, whereas a large number of the issues that hamper good selling will be lodged between investors' ears. So let us examine those two sets, the external first.

To begin, two aspects of optimism make selling difficult. At a macro level, middle- and upper-class people, especially in the United States, have a very positive life experience and live what's commonly known as classic American optimism. They literally live and own the American dream. Then, too, the entire process of investing—whether it be building a lemonade stand, directly investing in plant and equipment, or secondarily investing via securities—is based on affirmative or positive assumptions: growth, success, profit, the idea that "this will work." Buying, or investing, is a yes or a go, and selling is a no or a stop. Selling is thus a bit countercultural. And social stigma attaches to being branded a negative person.

Buying is done in optimism, in hope of great things, as an opening of a door to possibilities for wealth and profit and perhaps, more subtly, to the ego satisfaction of being proved right. Buying thus represents the positive end of the pain/pleasure spectrum, leaving selling at the other end. From our earliest days as children we have been taught to avoid sources of actual or possible pain. Selling, whether price is up or down, seemingly is always done under stress. Even when we do sell at a nice profit, it's with a palpable nagging fear (perhaps a bit of paranoia or persecution complex) that we're probably making a mistake; that we surely can't possibly be totally right, that as a slap in our face, this stock will go higher. And, of course, selling a stock when it is down occurs either in times of widespread fear and panic or at a moment of personal resignation to loss and admission that we were not as smart or as lucky as we'd thought. Thus, whether up or down, selling feels like a no-winner, so our first instinct is to flee from it.

Selling is also complexified by the unintentional but real daily conditioning we receive at the hands of the news media. Sometimes I'm amazed at what sheep we can be. One evening our favorite network anchor reporter tells us the market rose because investors were impressed by strong economic indicators; the very next night he or she intones that the market fell because investors fear that strong growth will bring the Federal Reserve Bank (the Fed) to raise interest rates. We'll sit there and bob our heads in "understanding" approval at both versions. In any event, the media's first function, as Alexander Cockburn said, is to confirm existing prejudice rather than to contradict it. We hear over and over how strong the economy is or, in recession, how badly things are going. All this reinforcement helps us to believe in current trends. Reinforcement of the well-known evidence conditions us to dismiss other scenarios. Repetition of yesterday's reasons lulls us into a comfort zone of fuzzy thinking or nonreasoning. We perceive that we are aligned with reality, so we see no reason to take action toward change. Thus we become biased, subtly but strongly, toward holding and against selling.

Those investors advised by full-service brokers also get a slanted number of buy versus sell advices. One study cited in the *American Association of Individual Investors* (AAII) *Journal* recently said there are about eight "buy" recommendations for every "sell" advice. Research departments are cost centers and so in most brokerage firms must be politically correct by never using the S-word, especially when related to actual or potential corporate finance clients. So they employ some classic euphemisms rather than actually saying "sell." It is probably an ultimate irony that the most commonly used alternative advice, "hold," literally has the opposite apparent intended meaning. One must understand the foreign tongue known as brokerage-ese. Other common translations of the word *sell,* roughly in order of faintness of praise implied, include the following:

- Accumulate
- Long-term buy
- Market performer
- Market weight
- Perform in line

- Underperform
- Underweight

The economics of a buy recommendation are much more favorable than those for a sell; the mathematics of the situation is straightforward. Putting aside the institutional risk of lost business from corporate clients, individual brokers can approach all investors for whom a purchase recommendation is appropriate but can do business on a sale advice with only that minority who already own the issue. Investors feel inadequate on money matters and so seek experts—or at least perceived experts. There are plenty to offer apparent assistance buying, but very few when the question is holding versus selling.

Another external obstruction to selling, because it makes clear thought more difficult, is information overload. Rumination in the stillness of a Vermont winter has its advantages. The Internet, granting its benefits, probably is exacerbating this overload problem. It is understandable to feel torn apart by all the what-ifs and yes-buts involved in selling because the world is not a simple linear experience. The nightly news alone will note five economic indicators, often giving a three-to-two verdict, and all just one-month readings cited entirely out of context. Investors who subscribe to a few advisory services and a telephone hotline and then watch CNBC or Bloomberg TV and visit a couple of investor Internet chatrooms can easily get multiple, somewhat differing opinions on one question: hold versus sell. The verdict is more likely to be 60/40 than 90/10; our natural tendency under such conditions of uncertainty (particularly in a period of stress) is to pull back, unconvinced that the case for selling is clear. The course of lesser resistance is to take *in*action, and hold. Investors today, more than ever before, are so plugged in and interactive and media overloaded and busy, that it is nigh impossible to find or to make time for quiet reflection and perspective.

Three pieces of loaded information that investors always carry around, for each holding, are disruptive because they are simultaneously vivid and irrelevant: the stock's all-time high, its highest price since purchase, and one's personal buy price. History has already proved the all-time high to have been at least a temporary mistake, one still being corrected. And the highest price reached since one has owned that prized "International Leisure Suit Industries"? That price represents a once-was and could-easily-be-again, and then it somehow morphs into an oughtta-be, gotta-be, deserves-to-be target. Each holder has his or her own view of a stock's deserved price, a private frame of reference unrelated to and unknown by other market participants. And one's personal purchase price becomes self-defined as a dividing line in the sand, between shame and denial and regret and perhaps stubbornness when a paper loss develops and pride and vindication and satisfaction and celebration after the stock rises above cost. Each investor measures his or her hopes and expectations for a stock using his or her personal, arbitrary purchase price as a base of reference, although that price is irrelevant to the rest of the market. (Relative exceptions exist at price levels where huge volumes of stock were exchanged, and these are of some importance as resistance or support levels to technical analysts.) However, a meaningful price goal for a stock should be based on fundamentals or on a technical-action target rather than on a percentage gain from any investors' random/ arbitrary purchase price. But the egocentric approach too often prevails inside investor's heads.

Selective memory also causes problems. Almost every investor has held a long-sleeping dog, only to finally sell it out of boredom or to offset some current taxable gains, without a fresh look at the fundamentals. The nightmare scenario is the one stock that was sold near what proved to be its lows and that then rose from the dead like Lazarus. That isolated incident becomes a private lifetime excuse for believing that almost any troubled company can rise from the dead. That wistful or persecution-complex hope is dangerous to investors' wealth, as technology moves ever faster and competition is now global. Digital Equipment ran some interesting TV commercials bearing an accidental nugget of investment truth. The commercials evoked the rapid and ceaseless change in computer environments and thus the personal risk of each purchase decision, saying, "In business, each of us will have many visions of the future; unfortunately most of them will turn out to have been wrong." That is perhaps a more profound restatement of a former research director's reminder to us analysts: companies have two kinds of managements, those who have faced adversity and those who will.

Another dangerous behavior that individual investors exhibit (and this has been observed repeatedly in visits with chapters of the American Association of Individual Investors nationwide), is not being careful enough when investing locally. There is nothing inherently wrong with local companies, whether on the Boston area's Route 128 or in California's Silicon Valley. But the investor adopts a local frame of reference that creates a comfort zone because the company's a big nearby employer about which there is considerable local buzz and media coverage, so it becomes all too easy to lose sight of the forest for the trees. The company is viewed as a great corporate citizen, for giving to a walk against hunger and for recycling. Local icons in the Boston area of recent vintage have been Digital Equipment, Prime Computer, and Wang Laboratories—and Waltham Watch and the Providence & Worcester Railroad in a previous generation. This appears to be an example of unfounded projection, in which a particular belief is held because of one's personal experience and/or conditioning. The holder of the belief then unconsciously expects that the rest of the investing populace will see the world (in this case, the revered local company) in the same favorable light.

Figures 3.1, 3.2, and 3.3 illustrate the hoped-for course of a stock price driven by forever-rising fundamentals, as seen by the buy-and-hold adherents, versus the reality of constantly and sharply fluctuating prices in the shorter term, driven by emotions and news. Figure 3.3 highlights two points: First, true investment reality is not the smooth line of ever-rising fundamentals; surprises happen. Second, negative surprises almost always carry greater costs than the rewards of positive surprises because fear outweighs greed and because people have an uneven psychological calculus regarding pain and pleasure.

There is abroad in the land a major bias in favor of buying and holding forever (at present buttressed by the consistent reinforcement of a long bull market that began in August 1982). There is a kernel of

Figure 3.1 Timing versus holding long term.

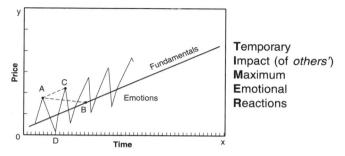

Temporary
Impact (of *others'*)
Maximum
Emotional
Reactions

Figure 3.2 Ways of viewing risk.

Mentally re-label
the *y*-axis as "RISK."

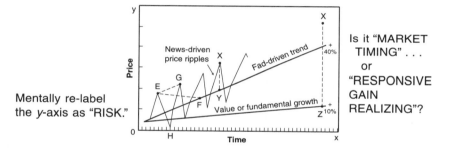

Is it "MARKET
TIMING" . . .
or
"RESPONSIVE
GAIN
REALIZING"?

Figure 3.3 Fundamentals and discounting rate determine value.

Temporary
Impact (of *others'*)
Maximum
Emotional
Reactions

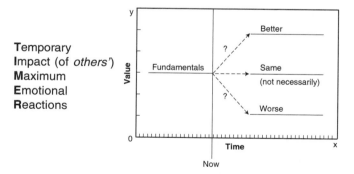

WHICH direction of changing assumptions carries most risk?

truth here if one owns an index fund at least as broad as the Standard & Poors (S&P) 500: the Ibbotson studies indicate that all U.S. stocks average a 10 to 11 percent gain per year over very long measurement periods. But that is of scant help when we focus on any single stock, in any specific present short time frame, and must decide whether to hold or to sell. Mutual funds' marketeers have history on their side on average when they urge buying and holding. What is interesting and thought provoking is that the fund investor's holding interminably assures a flow of annual 1 percent fees to the management company, whereas the typical portfolio manager turns over a conservative growth-and-income fund's holdings about 55 to 60 percent a year and thus does not practice the buy-and-hold religion.[2] Reality is that few can know in advance which will be the Coca-Colas and which the Hires Root Beers. Hindsight is easier than divining today which biotechnology start-up company will survive to conquer cancer.

If one had bought and held the seven then-largest U.S. computer companies in 1984, 10 years later that investor would have lost money in all of them—in the leading industry of our age and during a great bull market. Reality is that fundamentals drive stock prices in the very long term, but investors live in a string of todays, wherein right now new data and resulting emotional reactions of increasingly sharp intensity are setting prices in the short term. Investors and traders know all the reasons a stock is suddenly way up (and at that moment it feels wonderful and evokes feelings of grandiosity to be an owner), so it feels 100 percent counterintuitive to sell when the price is up. When a stock has been pounded by bad news and one painfully knows all about it, it is a courageous act to look beyond the present distress and to hold; so investors are likely to sell at just the point of maximum negative news or opinion impact. At both the highs and the lows, the investor is literally exposed to maximum external and vivid stimulus. I find it useful as an action screen to ask how the news could possibly get any better, which in cold logic is literally required for sustaining

---

[2]While the author is employed by Lipper Analytical Services, Inc., any views expressed herein are his personally and do not reflect the positions of that firm.

buying pressure and pushing prices even higher. That thinking discipline helps the nonpassive, analytical investor to sell when and because prices are suddenly and pleasantly up!

With the perverse exception of brief occasional selling climaxes, the external environment creates no sense of urgency to sell. And that helps investors succumb to a natural inertia. The game continues tomorrow. While a serious analyst would hesitate to compare investing to an outing to the racetrack, one aspect makes the races a less difficult game. The race ends; the final answer is indisputable. To continue in the game at the track, one must now make a new choice of which horse to ride for the next race or the next day. In the market, the bell rings and the race is freeze-framed until the next morning's opening. That construct, that different set of rules, creates a framework in which it is very easy to stay with an old nag even if it has fallen many, many lengths behind.

The external environment also biases investors against selling because of a tendency toward "analysis/paralysis" in this scientific and data-intense age. Although (or perhaps because!) there exists so much information relating to one's stock and its industry and to the condition of the overall economy and stock market, the investor vaguely feels never quite fully informed and therefore adopts the mad scientist's approach, looking for just that one more piece of information that will finally unlock the puzzle, solve the equation, and produce the absolutely correct answer. But while that extra data morsel is being retrieved, the environment itself has changed, creating the temptation to look for yet one more nugget, and thus it develops by default that one becomes a long-term holder one day at a time. Investors face a similarly bewildering set of potentially conflicting plus-and-minus factors when deciding whether to buy, and yet somehow at that juncture indecision is overcome and one places the order. No doubt persuasion and optimism enable the purchase decision.

Resentment that it costs additional money to correct a mistake, whether one's own or the broker's, also favors inaction, or holding over selling. For those who use deep-discount brokers, the news is becoming even better. With many live brokers charging $20 or less per trade and on-line firms charging less than half that, a round-trip commission is suddenly in the $10 to $40 range, or on a very few hundred shares literally less than one-eighth point. The dollar cost of changing one's mind can be that low! The cost of waiting until one has developed more information, or gets up courage from a crowd that has moved the stock several points, is, literally, several points! A one-eighth round trip makes commissions a nonissue. Commission phobia, like tax phobia, is really a smokescreen for not wanting to take action, a case of inertia caused by any in a whole range of internal factors. The truth is that every investor knew the rules in advance: one would pay commissions to play—and taxes to win!

Selling requires an investor to deal successfully with cognitive dissonance, and that is always difficult and stressful. This problem operates at two levels: First, the owner of a stock has formed a positive set of images and expectations. Selling requires processing new negative information and accepting its importance to the extent that one can internalize (and then act on!) a 180-degree reversal of one's prior thinking; selling often also requires putting aside some contrary current positive factors. Yesterday this was a great company with sound prospects, selling at a reasonable price, which the investor was brilliant enough to have bought lower and held through thick and thin to today's higher prices. Today, to sell, he or she must suddenly believe the company to be less attractive, having lost its future allure, and now overpriced based on the available information. One must usually concede having been, or having become, wrong in order to exit now. This is a construct loaded with many layers of emotional difficulty, to say the least!

Second, in order to sell well, the inhabitant of a mass culture and a mechanistic/scientific age must do what feels lonely and illogical—sell when everyone else palpably loves the stock and when all the news is patently positive. To sell means voluntarily deciding to part with something that has been treasured and loved (because it strokes the ego) and that has in fact treated the investor well. The longer the holding period, of course, the more powerful becomes this inertial force favoring holding.

One final somewhat external factor bears mention, although it is one the investor him- or herself has introduced through past action: If one made a mistake in judgment or suspended judgment and fell victim to mass psychology and bought out of greed or in excitement from powerful positive stimuli, one bought the stock high, and so now faces selling at a loss. A loss represents multiple subtle and complex nonmonetary problems. In brief, buying badly makes selling even more difficult!

The last few points have begun crossing a fuzzy border between the external and the internal, which are sometimes intertwined. So let us formally proceed now to the internal. Let me remind you that my training and focus is in finance rather than in psychology: this implies that you may need to fill in some nuances of implications of the information perceived and described in the following paragraphs. Nevertheless, even the untrained but observant investment analyst can see that at least some major aspects of selling put it in direct conflict with our basic urges, instincts, and desires.

To begin, we shall list a few inside-our-heads things that work at odds with selling, or at least with selling successfully. A number of these are entire subdisciplines on which extensive literature exists. In trying to analyze and categorize what is observed, one comes to conclude that nearly all the behaviors associated with refraining from selling (that is, with holding) are things we expect will serve to reduce or avoid pain. Let us then begin by naming a few attitudes and behaviors that directly or proactively support holding one's existing investments.

There was an old warhorse of a behavioral experiment at Princeton University in which two groups of students valued the beer mug differently depending on whether they held it or did not during the experiment. More of those who held it chose the mug over cash as their compensation than those who observed it from a distance. What is our own, we prize—even if for no special or logical reason. Otherwise garage sales could virtually replace all new, nongrocery, retail activity for many months, sparking a new great depression. Selling a stock that we hold starts out per se with one strike against it. My advice for an antidote is that investors view every stock as "cash" temporarily masquerading as a stock certificate, because any stock can become cash immediately. One must remember that the object of the investing game is to end up with *more cash*.

Here is still another phenomenon: investors appear to more strongly resist selling suggestions than buying ones. Buy advices focus on neutral territory, that vast area of stocks one does not presently own, whereas selling advice is a direct attack on what the investor or his or her ancestors have previously and actively chosen to acquire and then retain. Besides honoring our or their choices, holding represents remaining in the relative comfort of the perceived known versus the unknown: this company versus some other one (following a stress-inducing purchase-decision process).

When one owns a winner, the bond is even stronger: it tends to become adopted as a member of the family or as a beloved pet. It becomes "our Microsoft" or, to borrow a current Madison Avenue phrase, "my McDonalds." Affiliation with an investment winner is like being seen in the company of the captain of the football team or the prettiest cheerleader: one gains reflected glory. So the owner of a winner finds it very difficult to voluntarily terminate that bond. Owning the stock of a company that has prospered, especially over a long period, builds up a huge comfort zone for the shareholder. When the general market declines and carries a beloved stock down with it, one can take solace in remembering how the price bounced back from earlier setbacks like 1987 or 1990 or early 1994 and went on to new heights of glory.

Or if the drop is really painful, one can conveniently take solace in the fundamental greatness of the company, for example, 27 successive years of rising dividends. One asserts that a company this great clearly should not trade at just 9x EPS (earnings per share)—assuming that one is old enough to remember single-digit price/earnings (P/E) ratios. If and when the market bounces back and if indeed the company's growth record remains intact, all is once again well; so the

41

investor can subconsciously score a point for fundamentals and the concept of "buy and hold."

Typically, investors erroneously transfer their attitudes toward or their perceptions of the company onto the stock itself. It is precisely here where the trap of holding forever regardless of price comes into existence. Coca-Cola is a great company. It has clear prospects for future growth in the less-developed world. But on what realistic basis can one justify 45x earnings for under-20 percent growth? The company is so great and its stock has treated the investor so well that he or she cannot imagine or visualize actually selling it. So, in the next bear market such investors are predestined to ride this great company's stock all the way down. In such patterns of behavior, the holder has literally confused the company with the stock. (In addition, one subconsciously sets up the previous high price as a standard of "value," which creates a reference point difficult to abandon; selling requires giving up that marker.) A stock's price is merely a scoreboard, a barometer, of the present collective attitudes of other investors toward the company and, in the current "momentum" market phase, toward the stock itself. But price is not the same as value! Price functions for each investor personally in two ways: It quickly signals the amounts of one's profits and of one's wealth as the stock rises. But it also acts internally as an indictor of one's brilliance in buying and holding this position. Holding functions to keep a pleasant ego stroker readily at hand. Switching to another stock would force the investor to take the chance of not surely or soon replacing this comfort-granting friend. Stroking the investor's ego is no small matter. Those who own a stock spend considerable time reading about it—in many cases, at least in the early phases until comfort is firmly established, as much as or more time than prior to effecting the purchase. It pleases and comforts the holder to find articles reciting how well the company or the stock has done, and one is thrilled to discover some new angle or reason not previously known or imagined. Aha! One suddenly is even smarter than one had thought! And, look, Warren Buffett or Jimmy Rodgers or Peter Lynch likes it. Holding a winner keeps the investor securely in a growing comfort zone. Such holders stand ready to defend the honor of their holdings, ever assuming they continue to have all the virtue they had when first encountered and when living together was begun. Holders are ready to debate any nonbelievers! Of course, their egos are involved. Once a stock has been purchased, its owner/holder filters news to comport with the preestablished positive opinion. For example, two people read about a company laying off 2,500 employees to cut costs. The nonholder celebrates her or his wisdom in not investing in that difficult industry, while the holder sees a brighter side—next quarter's margins will start a pattern of improvement! This way of interacting with the news surrounding one's holdings functions to boost the ego further when a stock is up or to shield the ego when price is down. This self-serving process of personal self-affirmation creates an unfair trial for the stock, which is almost guaranteed to emerge with a "not guilty" verdict.

Selling also subconsciously involves the process of coming to closure, usually a painful one. Many closures or passages in life are sad ones: packing up to leave classmates and the familiar scenes of our alma mater upon graduation; at last ending a long-nonfunctional marriage with the finality of a divorce—a public and official admission of a failure; cleaning out great-grandmother's attic after she's gone to a rest home or to her final rest; burying a dear friend or professional colleague. There is a profound finality about all these closures. As a devout baseball fan, I find the annual ritual of the World Series a near-mystical experience. And its end makes vivid the feelings closure generates. A few minutes after the final out of the final game, the television camera pans to the losing team's dugout: several players, particularly the veterans, stare out in sadness and regret at the playing field, imagining what they could have done better to avert the now-official verdict of personal and undeniable loss. That is the type of emotion that finality conjures up in us, and we do not like it very much.

Selling means that we personally have acted to set the final score, and we will be reminded of our decision and its consequences when the computer sends us our trade confirmation and again next April when the time arrives to fill out Schedule D. Buying opens a whole range of possibilities, but selling ends any chance for revision of the outcome. Ours is an extremely tolerant and nonjudgmental society where almost anything is all right. Some religions and schools teach that there is no real right or wrong. Corporate and government bureaucracies make decisions in slow and deliberative ways and often couch the result in softening terms. "We have reconsidered and revised our policy in light of new inputs" covers for "We made a real bad mistake." Too many people refuse to accept responsibility and seek to sue everyone in sight when something goes wrong. Selling, especially if at a loss, has the investor saying very bluntly, "I was wrong or am no longer right." That statement is highly judgmental and jars our beveled-edged sensibilities.

Even when an investor indeed does have a nice paper profit at hand, the seemingly natural course is to shrink back from selling because one just knows, from past experience and perhaps from listening to a small paranoid voice, that as soon as it is sold, this stock will slap him or her in the face and move higher. It almost certainly will happen on the very next tick, or perhaps at next Friday's close, or next year's price; so the investor is virtually sure of facing future feelings of shame at being wrong sometime, if he or she now takes action to sell. The possibilities of being similarly wrong are equally there at the instant one buys, but the essential openness of that dynamic allows one to accept those chances. Selling, on the other hand, would close a book that one could decide to leave open. Thus, a retreat into inaction is the easiest course of behavior.

The vignette in the preceding paragraph captures the essential features of perfectionism, an increasingly pervasive cultural force in our computerized and monitored lives. The workplace demands zero defects on penalty of possible dismissal. One's children simply must be admitted into the top-tier preschools or their lives are already pointing toward the ash heap. Our sports teams, professional or collegiate, must win that championship each year or someone will answer for it. In the stock market, the putative, coolly logical, random walker should see a sale as a 50/50 choice. But in the world of warm-blooded human beings, investors value pain more acutely than gain, so selling is an underdog choice. The odds of being wrong, by at least an eighth, are so high when we sell, that one flees from this chance at self-humiliation. Humiliation is a very strongly avoided experience, as illustrated by the surveys that until recently (when snakes took over as #1) placed "fear of having to speak in public" above "fear of death." (Read that again and reflect for a moment!)

Perfectionism, it should also be noted in fairness, also operates powerfully at the time of deciding about purchasing an investment. U.S. investors are now confronted with over 10,000 different mutual funds, before even counting the 6,000 extra classes of shares. Even if one manages not to inhale deeply when reading the January magazine issues, the odds are incredibly high against choosing the single biggest winner, even within any major asset class. It is my personal view that people's heightened perception of the chance of failing to be perfect is a factor supporting the explosion of index funds and probably also helps to explain the rising popularity of funds of funds, wrap accounts, and now life-cycle funds. The last offer the chance to buy once and then never need to worry about when to switch out, because by their nature these new funds gradually change like chameleons such that their portfolios gracefully become more conservative over the years as their (buy-and-) holders age.

Perhaps yet another of the many reasons investors incrementally dislike selling decisions (versus buying ones) is that selling and raising cash usually brings with it the need for a second, additionally stress-inducing buy decision. Non-full-time investors, we who are in the profession should not forget, do not eat and breathe and love this process on which we daily thrive—they abhor and fear it!

Each buying and likewise each selling decision introduces the possibility of both success and failure. But of course buying decisions merely open the game, leaving the result an open-ended unknown. Selling decisions offer no such comfort, for they seal the verdict forever. Those readers trained in the mysterious ways of the mind know well the syndromes of fear of failure and fear of success. Selling at a gain leaves chances for both (failure if the stock goes higher), and selling at a loss seals a verdict of failure (and maybe twice, if the price then rebounds!)

Aversion to admission of failure is extremely wrong, to the point of overwhelming logic. Several years ago, as an analyst with a retail brokerage firm, I followed but had never recommended Ideal Basic Cement, once a bulwark of the Colorado economy but lately trading at $1.50 a share. Literally all its holders had losses. A Swiss company that had previously provided a temporary bailout now wanted to buy the rest of the company and offered $1 a share—yes, a takeover offer not above but below current market! The original controlling family was planning to vote for and thus seal the deal. Yet a number of brokers indicated they absolutely could not move their clients to sell to avoid the certain further one-third loss of capital! Some shareowners had bought or inherited the stock with a cost basis of $20 or $30, so for them a sale had for several years been more valuable for its unlockable tax-loss cash value than for the remaining principal. Yet they were unmovable. The previously cited volume on the mysteries of successful selling also mentions another company, Johns Manville, which emerged from bankruptcy and reverse split its shares one-for-eight. The old stock was trading at $2 and the new shares trading "when issued" at $8, not $16. Anyone could literally see a 50 percent further loss coming, and yet some holders refused to let their brokers sell them out! They could, by analogy, read the box score of tomorrow's ballgame in advance and yet still wanted to bet on the wrong team. How deeply ingrained is the tendency to myopic loss aversion!

Behavioral experiments have consistently demonstrated that people place higher value on a loss of a given amount than on a gain of the same amount, that is, pain avoidance overmatches pleasure seeking. This would explain why people hold on to their losers or their "snoozers" rather than cash out and move the proceeds into a more promising alternative. A recent article by Richard Thaler of the University of Chicago described a proposed coin-flipping game that paid more for wins than it cost for losses. He invited a finance-professor colleague, who clearly understood the game's positive net worth, to play—but only once—for a $125 win against a $100 loss. The answer was a refusal. The same colleague, when asked if willing to play 100 times and settle up only at the finale, agreed with a single condition: "As long as you don't make me watch." Pain avoidance, even in the face of known eventual pleasure, is that strong. So selling at a loss or selling when one fears a future opportunity loss is strongly distasteful! There is probably subtly much more than meets the eye to mutual fund marketeers' suggestions not to watch the price every day and to focus on the long term.

Of course, continuing to hold can readily and conveniently reflect the process of denial, on which there exists a considerable literature. The cycle of stock prices maps onto people's emotional responses. In the first phase of a decline from a major top, investors experience disbelief, which can be seen as another way of describing *denial.* Denial is a wonderfully handy, although ultimately dysfunctional, protector of the ego. Denial starts the process of rationalization that allows an investor to hold without much discomfort, rather than sell, a position that isn't working. It works until the loss is deep or lingering, at which point one must find another crutch such as *rationalization.* This latter behavior underlies the age-old switch-of-objectives maneuver. Imagine a trader having bought California Widgetronics at $10 on rumors it would be taken over three weeks later at $17 by a large Asian conglomerate. Not merely three weeks but three-fourths of a year has passed and prospects for such a workout are now nil; Cal Widget has become the veritable Midget Widget, trading at $6 rather than $17. Yet our would-be scalper holds on. Asked why, he will respond that the company has a great R&D (research-and-development program, supports the green movement in its recycling efforts, and, with rebounding values of West Coast realty, has a parking lot alone worth over $4 per share. The disappointed speculator, unwilling to admit defeat, has become a long-term "value investor" through the back door. How did that happen? Rationalization; refusal to admit a mistake; hesitancy to come to closure, avoidance of pain; ego protection.

Having listened to literally thousands of individual investors, I have heard numerous tales about troublesome stocks. It is difficult to escape the hypothesis that deciding to refrain from selling is actually a defiant act of ego in an age in which people so often feel emasculated and powerless. Congress controls taxes; employers wield ultimate power over their job security; and they might be struck down by lightning on the fairway or by an 18-wheeler on the highway. But here's one place an investor does retain final authority and control: against all advice and logic, he or she can hold on to this greyhound puppy that matured into a basset hound merely by saying no to selling. (It might boost one's injured ego to exercise that power.)

And, ultimately, holding is so much easier than selling because holding as a default is an expression of procrastination, yet another psychologically rooted behavior, which has its own rich literature.

Is there a simple cure for the ingrained and self-destructive aversion to selling? Perhaps two practices can help in the battle against those forces that make selling so difficult. Both, not surprisingly, require the exercise of self-discipline.

First, before a stock is purchased, a clear selling-price target should be established on the basis of three interacting factors: (1) a price target (P), driven by (2) a scenario (S), and not least importantly, within (3) a time frame (T). The resulting combination "PST!" can serve as a mentally whispered reminder. If all three elements are not present, the stock position will leave its owner's money floating aimlessly; no means of evaluating success/failure or of coming to closure will exist. (Unless one's actual articulated goal is to pass the entire estate to the heirs, logically stocks are bought for the purpose of being sold!) Then, having price target and underlying logic in mind and in writing, at the slightest temptation to change the rules investors need to put themselves on the couch and take extensive notes on their selling-versus-holding behavior. Everyone has one or more recurring sell/hold behavior patterns; becoming aware of these (a checklist on every trade is suggested) enables sidestepping self-created potholes that keep investors for otherwise unknown reasons holding when they really ought to be selling. A practical discipline that overcomes several of the self-defeating tendencies described in the preceding paragraphs is to place a sell order at the target price immediately when the stock is purchased.

Second, investors should apply a critical test to each holding–and I recommend that this be done frequently: Knowing what they now do (not what they originally hoped or expected), and looking at today's price, they should ask, "If I had extra cash and it would not violate portfolio balance, would I buy this stock right now at its current price?" If they would not, the logical conclusion is that it should not be retained in the portfolio because holding is actually just redeploying capital by default into the currently held stock for another day or another week or longer, without phoning the broker or paying a commission. What they would not buy at the current price they should not hold (holding being just reinvestment for another day), so that stock must be sold. This is a harsh but valid discipline. Clearly, with all the difficulties surrounding selling described in these few allotted pages, any new disciplines or aids to overcoming the real and psychological problems investors face in this area should be of value.

CHAPTER 4

The Psychology of Picking Stocks

Matthew M. Stichnoth

Believe it or not, the psychology involved in picking undervalued stocks isn't nearly as complicated as, say, the psychology surrounding picking wallpaper for your kitchen. Rather, it essentially involves resolving a single, exquisite dilemma that's illustrated in the following story:

> A policeman is walking his beat on a dark, foggy night. He comes to a corner, at which stands a single street lamp that throws off just enough light to provide a small beacon in the surrounding shadows. At the base of the lamp is a man on all fours. He's evidently drunk and certainly soaked, and he's staring at the pavement.
>
> The patrolman approaches the poor sot and asks what he's doing. The man looks up briefly. "I'm looking for my keys!" he answers quickly, then gets back to work.
>
> So the policeman starts to look, too. The two poke around for a couple of minutes until finally the cop, thinking he might narrow the search, asks exactly where the man has lost his keys.
>
> "A couple of blocks over, near North and Main," he replies.

"A couple of blocks over! But if you lost your keys *there*, then why are you looking for them *here?*"

"What, are you kidding? The light's so much better here!"

The incident shows perfectly the misbegotten process through which most people go as they try to find undervalued stocks. The fact of the matter is that most investors (with good reason, as you'll soon read) would prefer to eat ground glass than to seek overlooked values in the places in which those values are most likely to be found.

Rather, people prefer to stick with what they know—to stick near the lamp post—whether it's effective or not. On Wall Street, that means that people rely on stock-picking techniques that, although useless, are nonetheless comfortable and reassuring.

Over the course of the discussion that follows, I'll examine how it is that the typical investor has gotten into this fix and what he or she might do to get out of it. I'll first briefly discuss Wall Street's culture of *contrarianism*, and show that it is more central to successful investing than many investors—notably the new, 1990s-era, mutual fund crowd—might realize. Second, I'll discuss *avoidance techniques* that have been concocted over the years that let investors *think* they're being contrarians when they're really not; and I'll dwell on one in particular that's especially counterproductive. And third, I'll present some shorthand techniques that can allow investors to find *real* values without having to endure an inordinate amount of psychological stress.

CONTRARIANISM

To start at the beginning, Wall Street's "culture of contrarianism" is older and more deep-rooted than even its yen for Brooks Brothers suspenders. The notion behind the culture, of course, is the soul of simplicity: always and everywhere, Wall Street lore goes, markets go to extremes and must necessarily self-correct over time.

It is a notion that is as old as the buttonwood tree, and it goes like this. First, a small group of investors will come to a tentative investment conclusion (e.g., Cabbage Patch Kids could end up being a popular item at Christmas) and will invest in a number of stocks that figure to benefit. Then as that tentative conclusion shows early signs of being correct, Cabbage Patch-related stocks will start to rise, and other investors will also show interest.

But in order to justify their investments, the second wave of buyers will likely have higher expectations of eventual Cabbage Patch profitability than the initial wave did. Next, those new higher expectations will be borne out, too. Then more people will become investors on the basis of expectations that are even more hopeful.

You've seen the pattern thousands of times. And you know, too, what happens in the end: eventually, there will be a great horde of bulls who are wildly hopeful—they will have convinced themselves that at least one Cabbage Patch doll will be given to every man, woman, and child in the country at Christmas—while the pool of incremental buyers of the Cabbage Patch stocks dwindles down to nearly nothing. Sooner or later, the sky-high consensus view will be shown to be way overdone, often at the very moment that the pool of incremental stock buyers dries up once and for all. And then—c-c-crack!—the whole mess will come crashing down.

It occurs as regularly as the sunrise, and the investor with the courage and insight to stand against the growing crowd just as expectations peak stands to make an enormous amount of money. Similarly (and more commonly) the investor who steps in to buy just as consensus expectations reach low tide can scoop up some astonishing bargains.

This is the essence of investing, you are saying to yourself. And you are right; for even though the notion of contrarian investing has become a semi-exotic investment concept in the all-bullish stock market environment of the 1990s, the fact of the matter is that *all* investment styles, no matter how modish, are really dressed-up contrarianism.

The momentum player, for example, bets on quarterly earnings surprises on the assumption (unspoken or not) that the consensus view, no matter how bullish, still isn't bullish enough. The growth-at-a-reasonable-price maven, meanwhile, is implicitly saying that the market has fundamentally misjudged his or her favorite companies' earnings growth and visibility. Even the most rock-solid investor of them all, Mr. Buy-and-Hold, must believe that no matter what the consensus might think, nothing terminal will ever happen to *his* companies.

THE UNPLEASANTNESS OF CONTRARIANISM

We are all contrarian investors, therefore, whether we want to be or not. And this is fine, as far as it goes. Unfortunately, the idea of having a market full of individuals who are all spoiling for a fight is sort of nutty. Most people by their nature prefer *not* to not get swept along and aren't all that comfortable standing up and disagreeing with the crowd, especially if they happen to be in the middle of it. If anything, just the opposite is true: individuals get swept along by groups all the time (which is why, for instance, things like political bandwagons and lynch mobs have been known to occur).

Not so surprisingly, therefore, true down-and-dirty contrarian investing can be *hugely* unpleasant and extremely difficult to do right. If you doubt it, look at Microsoft Corporation. In theory, Microsoft ought to be a contrarian's dream: if it is not the best-loved company in the country, it is certainly the best known and most admired. The mighty Bill Gates is as famous as Madonna, is much richer, and seems to have taken a long-term lease on the cover of *Fortune* magazine. In the meantime, the stock is trading at 15 times its current-year sales, 16 times yearend book value, and—get this!—52 times current-year earnings. Of the 28 analysts who cover the stock, 22 have investment ratings that are either highly bullish (10 analysts) or modestly bullish (12 analysts). There is just one "sell" recommendation, and it is half-hearted.

There is virtually nobody anywhere, therefore, who's not enthralled with Microsoft. But you're a contrarian investor, remember. Given all the foregoing, how do you suppose it would feel to walk into a convention full of money managers (a great number of whom have made their careers by buying as much Microsoft as they could) and have to introduce yourself to each one and then add, "Oh, and I'm short 10,000 Microsoft and will be selling some more as soon as I get back to the office."

It might be a highly defensible contrary position to take (you might even want to emphasize that 15-times-revenue bit), but virtually everyone in the room will believe that you've lost your mind, and more than a few will tell you so. Others will simply laugh at you. And still others will scamper away as soon as they politely can and will ignore you for the rest of the evening. By the time you're finished meeting and greeting, nobody's going to even want to breathe your air.

All of this helps explain, in case you were still doubtful, why our friend the drunk didn't want to stray too far into the loneliness of the unknown to find his keys. But ironically, even though real, live, contrary-minded investing involves doing the things we hate most, just about every investor knows that he or she is supposed to be contrary-minded. Because of this tension, most investors take refuge in a number of techniques—they think of them as "avoidance devices"—that allow them to feel *as if* they're being genuine contrarians without having to go through the unpleasantness of actually *being* contrarian.

There must be dozens of ways to do this, from stock picking via astrology (yes, there are zodiacal mutual funds available), to "socially responsible" investing, to technical analysis. No, none are underhanded (or inordinately harmful, for that matter). They just don't do much good.

SCREENING FOR STOCKS

This gets us, at last, to the villain of the piece. To us, there is one avoidance device that stands out as being particularly noteworthy, both because it's used by just about every manager around and also because it's so hopelessly ineffective. No, we're not referring to an overreliance on sell-side research or to the popularity of the Super Bowl predictor. Rather, our favorite culprit is the use of desktop computers to screen for "cheap" stocks. As you'll read in a moment, not only does screening for stocks not lead to outperformance, it *can't* lead to it. Yet people do it anyway, slavishly, for the sake of their mental balance.

Oh, you know how the whole process works. Put a laundry list of parameters in one end of a computer (for instance, "Show me all companies that are trading at less than one times book value, that have shown revenue growth of at least 20 percent annually over the past three years, and that have debt less than 25 percent of capital"), then press a button and—poof!—out the other end comes a perfectly believable list of attractive-sounding stocks.

Makes perfect sense, right? You wonder why everybody doesn't do it—which, of course, is the problem. Everybody *does* do it, and in basically the same way. This is why so many managers lag the market. But then again, how could computer screens allow them to do anything but lag? Don't forget, after all, that the hundreds of thousands of analysts, strategists, and portfolio managers at work around the country sifting for stocks on their computers all must inevitably use just one of a few basic sets of screening parameters. After all, you can look for low-priced growth, or you can look for value, or you can look for earnings momentum. But in each case there are only so many ways that you can set screening parameters to define each set of stocks. Everybody, therefore, is looking at basically the same screen. How contrary-minded!

What's worse, though, is that they're all culling through exactly the same SEC-and-FASB-blessed data. And all that data is available at the same level of detail to everybody and is disclosed to the entire marketplace at *exactly the same time.* Oh, and everyone's computer is roughly of the same speed and power so that no one can out-number-crunch anybody else.

You see the problem. In the end, despite all the highfaluting inputs and the mounds and mounds of numbers, computer screening tends to give everybody the same lists of stocks all at once. What's the investment advantage in that?

And yet even though screening for stocks almost certainly does *not* lead to stock market outperformance (don't forget that 70 percent or more of all money managers underperform in any given year), money managers still screen obsessively. The reason? A main one, we would wager, is that it lets them feel as if they really are going against the crowd, but without having to endure all that unpleasantness.

INVESTING WITHOUT PAIN

The typical money manager is, therefore, in a quandary. Still, there are some ideas that we would offer that can enable investors to go invest against the consensus without all the psychic pain. They aren't foolproof, and they can't always be applied on a wide scale. Then again, they do seem to work, both theoretically and empirically. My ideas are:

1. *Insider buying.* Heavy buying by company insiders (especially by the Chief Executive Officer (CEO) can be a strong indication that the market has overdone its pessimism. And why not? Insiders know what's going on in their companies better than the market as a whole does. When insiders start to buy, therefore, it tends to be a good sign that bullish change is in the air. From a psychological standpoint, meanwhile, standing against the crowd shoulder to shoulder (figuratively anyway) with the CEO can be a real picker-upper. Caveat: watch out for companies that make stock-purchase loans to insiders on easy terms, and watch out, as well, for companies that require that officers own a certain amount of company stock.

2. *Spinoffs.* Spinoffs, by their very nature, tend to be prototypical stock market orphans. First of all, often the only reason a spinoff even *occurred* was that the spun-off company's ex-parent couldn't find a buyer for it in the first place. Failing a sale, then, the stock is unceremoniously distributed (usually as odd lots) to the ex-parent's holders, who in turn know nothing about it and who therefore have a strong predisposition to sell—which is usually what they do. In the meantime,

the stocks typically have no broad sponsorship, particularly among sell-side research departments. The result of all this is *low initial valuations*. What spun-off companies *do* have, however, are suddenly incentivized managements who often end up doing very big things for their shareholders. Anyway, combine the low-ball valuations with those revved-up managements and–surprise!–studies show that spinoffs tend to be big outperformers.

3. *Busted IPOs.* One of the good things about the ongoing boom in initial public offerings (IPOs) is that so many IPOs blow up soon after liftoff and become bona fide values. Oh sure, a lot of newly public companies aren't ready for prime time and deserve to be put in stock market limbo. Then again, a newly public company's problem might often be just a single oddball quarterly earnings report or a management that's still getting the knack of communicating with the Street. Yet even in those cases, the stocks of newly public companies will be tossed overboard and forgotten, even by (or *especially* by) the company's bankers. With no sponsorship, the stock can lie low for eons. Once the company's problems get fixed (and often the fixes are surprisingly easy), the stocks can become awfully attractive, whether anyone notices or not.

Okay, we'll grant you that you won't be able to run $10 billion on the basis of insider buying, spinoffs, and busted IPOs. (Then again, figuring out how to invest $10 billion is a very nice problem to have.) On the other hand, you can at least reap some of the rewards of ignoring the crowd without having to endure too much psychological pain. Not bad for a start.

CHAPTER 5

Psychopathology of
Everyday Investing

John Schott

Imagine you are walking on a city street, in a crowd, when suddenly you feel quite disoriented and notice something wrong with your vision. You think you may be having a stroke or maybe a heart attack.

If you're in a crowd and collapse or need help, it's very unlikely that anyone will help you. The most famous example of this is the murder of Kitty Genovese in New York: at least 38 people heard her screams and saw what was happening, yet not one person called the police. No one came to help.

Initially that was cited as an example of the alienation from modern society. How horrible to be in New York City where no one cared and no one would pay attention. Two social psychologists, Bill Latant and John Darley, have examined this problem and concluded it is a universal group phenomenon that no one steps forward. People are paralyzed. What someone in an emergency situation should do is say, "You with the checkered shirt, I think I'm having a stroke. I need your help right now." Thomas Moriarity demonstrated the success of this action in a well-known study when he showed that strangers asked to watch a person's belongings were approximately five times more likely to prevent a theft than people who had not been asked.

Social psychology looks at behavior from the standpoint of identifying the rules that govern our interchange. Psychoanalytic psychiatry looks at behavior from the standpoint of unconscious conflicts during early life development and the symptoms that develop because of them. Cognitive psychology looks at people's thoughts and the distortions in the thought process.

There is a great tendency in human beings to dichotomize; to be competitive; to try to see one idea as better than another, one group as better than another, one sex as better than another, rather than seeing differences and trying to put things together in some kind of syncretistic way. In the emerging field of behavioral economics we have reached a point at which it is important to keep an open mind, to receive all ideas, and to attempt to syncretize those ideas. It is dangerous to select a particular point of view as being the only one that can explain behavior.

Behavior is multidetermined and very complicated. This particular field, the psychology of investing, is in its infancy. Joseph Lakonishok is a leader in behavioral economics. Robert Cialdini is a behavioral economist who comes from a social psychology point of view. I am a psychoanalyst and come from that perspective. Together we resemble the fabled blind Hindu wisemen who each touched a different part of an elephant and, based on the one part, described the animal. We who represent the pioneers in exploring investment psychology are in the same predicament as the blind wisemen—each looking at the field from our own orientation.

There is a necessary preface to this paper, and it deals with the meanings of money, because the meanings of money are inextricably woven into the fabric of investing.

Paper money is the ultimate symbol. Although it has no intrinsic value of its own, it can purchase almost anything else of value, not only in a capitalistic society like our own, but in virtually every other society. Money has incredibly complex meanings. Money can buy an automobile. It can buy a house and health care. It cannot really buy love, but it can buy a certain degree of relationship. And it has power to it—both real power and symbolic power.

According to psychoanalytic theory, money is the unconscious equivalent of human excrement. This accounts for the many conflicts that surround money and also for the intense feelings of shame associated with money. These feelings are especially difficult when they revolve around money that a person thinks is undeserved, for example, money that is derived from a large inheritance or from a large lottery winning.

When I ask the question, "What are you worth?," most people begin to calculate—I have a house, I have a car, I have these assets, I have this much money in the bank, I have a retirement plan. They tally up their material worth, and then they subtract from that whatever their debt might be. Then they say, well, that's my net worth. In our society, if you ask that question in general, most people will interpret it that way: Their worth is the amount of money or assets that they have.

Such an estimate of worth comes from a competitive standpoint. It also comes from the notion in finance that the way the score is kept is in the number of dollars that you have. But "What are you worth?" might also mean: What kind of father are you? What kind of mother are you? "What kind of person are you? Do you live up to your ideals? Are you a religious person? How is your relationship with God? Do you do a good job at work? Do you do things to help other people? Have you made a great discovery?

I might think far more highly of myself if I were spending my time trying to conquer schizophrenia, rather than trying to figure out why people invest in a particular way. I try not to be too guilty about that because I really love the field, so I rationalize that following what one loves is a good thing.

Money has a tremendous libidinal value in society. Many people love money, overvalue money, and will do a great deal to obtain it. That is because we libidinize it to such an extent that it becomes, in a sense, a distortion for us. In this context, it loses its real meaning, that a certain amount of money can buy a certain amount of goods. Instead it symbolizes sexuality; self-worth; power; the ability to acquire relationships, to advance a career, or to become a politician; and many, many other things.

I don't want to overemphasize the psychoanalytic viewpoint on the meanings of money. There may be a difference of opinion about what the meanings of money are, but there is a uniformity of opinion among psychiatrists that money is loaded with meaning. Money connotes power and security to many people. Indeed, money does confer a certain measure of power, but not as much as is fantasized. Money also brings some sense of security, although in truth, in modern day America, the reality is that a sense of security is much more significantly determined by your health, by your relationships, by being in love with someone, and by your perceived relationship with God. So all of those things, in fact, contribute far more to a sense of security than the amount of money that you have in the bank. With that preface, I can now move to the market.

There are three essential qualities to sound investing: (1) knowledge—you have to know something about what you're doing; you can't just do the dartboard routine although as we know that can have pretty good results; (2) experience—there is no substitute for experience in investing; and (3) control of emotions.

Warren Buffett, in his introduction to Ben Graham's book *The Intelligent Investor,* said that to invest successfully over a lifetime does not require a stratospheric IQ, unusual business insights, or inside information. What is needed is a sound intellectual framework for making decisions and the ability to keep emotions from corroding that framework. Warren Buffett is a man with an astonishingly good investing record. I believe what has made Buffett so good is not only his brilliance about investing, but his unique ability to focus himself totally on the investment process while minimizing emotional involvement in it.

The truth is that most individual investors follow no investing plan and are very much prey to their emotions. Buy decisions are often made impulsively, and sell decisions are frequently made out of superstition, fear, anxiety, guilt, and masochism. A very common example of this is the investor who does just the opposite of Wall Street's maxim: Cut your losses, let your winners run. My research shows that investors who violate this maxim tend to have many obsessive personality traits. Obsessive people have a tendency to become so anxious when they own a stock rising in price that they impulsively sell at the first weakness, often rationalizing, "You never go broke taking a profit.: On the other hand, when such an obsessive person owns a stock dropping in price, they keep saying to themselves, "When it gets back to what I paid for it, I will sell it," Here are the mechanisms that I postulate are involved in this behavior. Obsessive people have a great deal of unconscious guilt from Oedipal strivings in childhood. If they have something that is going to make them successful, they feel a lot of anxiety associated with their aggressions. Thus they want to exit that situation as soon as possible. When they are losing money, their guilt is unconsciously expiated. So while they're consciously suffering, on an unconscious level they experience a form of moral masochism that it is unconsciously gratifying.

I recently tracked the investing habits of a group of volunteers who were willing to be interviewed and to take an MMPI, which we used to group them into obsessives or "normals." I took those who were normal as a control group, and those who had obsessive profiles as the obsessive group. I did my best to match them in terms of age, education, and income, and I followed them for a three-year investing period. Over that time, it was very clear (the difference was statistically significant) that the obsessive people were quicker to sell their stocks when prices were rising. Their holding period was short, and the amount of money made quite small.

On the other side, the normal group frequently tended to cut their losses short and when they didn't, they could articulate good reasons for holding. For example, they would say," This is a biotech company, and I know the people who are involved in it. It's going to take me five years to have a payoff, but I'm really going to come out of it in great shape." The obsessive group, on the other hand, suffered terribly, didn't sell, didn't have a reason for holding, and clung to the "I'll sell when it gets back to what I paid for it" notion. That notion is the psychological mechanism of undoing. The pain associated with the narcissistic injury of having made a mistake can be undone by a form of denial.

There is a great tendency on the part of obsessive people to use undoing as a defense mechanism. If they're cruel to their spouse, they will want to make that up in some way, or they will take it back. The injury has already been done, but they don't appreciate that. Instead, they attempt to undo it. The pattern persists in their investment practices. Similar neurotic patterns exist among other personality types. Depressed people are so convinced that they will lose their money that either they don't invest at all or they stick to bank accounts. Narcissistic people overidentify and stick to glamour stocks.

There are basically three current investment styles: value-investing, growth-investing, and momentum-investing. Growth-investing in the hands of a person like T. Rowe Price produces substantial profits. It is based on a psychology of greed and the belief that well-informed analysts can accurately predict earnings. Although accurate predictions are not possible much of the time, it is possible to recognize a good-quality, growing company and to buy at a reasonable price and hold. Exercised judiciously, especially when combined with dollar-cost averaging, growth-investing has produced excellent results. However, growth-investing requires more skill than either value-investing or momentum-investing. For growth-investing to do well, one has to have a sense of what the products are and an ability to make judgments about them. So if you come from a background that has the requisite skills to do that—an engineer looking at an engineering project, a physician looking at a drug—and you can bring that skill to bear while simultaneously controlling all of your psychological processes, you've got the makings of a good growth-stock investor. This requires more skill than does value-investing where you might follow set guidelines about selecting stocks based on low price/earnings (P/E) ratios, low price/sales ratios, low price/book ratios, and the like. Momentum-investing requires no brains, although a computer is helpful. Knowing what the product is may be a disadvantage. The idea of momentum-investing is buying stocks whose earnings are rising in the top 10 percent of all stocks *and* whose stock price is similarly rising.

Momentum-investing is the newest school of investing, and it just may turn out to be the most successful. Louis Navalliere's *MPT Review* and James Collins's *OTC Review* have been the most successful investing newsletters of recent years. Navalliere's actual money management performance—the translation of theory into practice—has also been superior, as has that of some other momentum managers. However, until there is a real bear market to test those theories, I'm going to suspend my own judgment. It's quite possible that momentum-investing may simply turn out to be the newest example of the greater fool theory.

However, if momentum theory is the new sliced bread, then the underlying psychological principle could have to do with psychological inertia. The mind tends to work in psychological sets, resisting change. Social psychologists call this phenomenon *consistency*. This has also been shown in studies about game theory. If people are taught one way, but then the game is rigged in a different way that should alter their behavior, they stubbornly stick to the first way. Studies by Lakonishok suggest that this inertia may create a systematic window of opportunity to buy or to sell before the market reacts to news. We will see in time, especially during the next bear market, whether momentum-investing is as powerful as it seems to be.

Let us now focus on the psychopathology of everyday investing. We all know that greed is the major emotion during bull markets and fear is the major emotion during bear markets. When the market is rising, investor expectations rise with it. The historical norm of 9.5 percent total return, compounded annually for equities, has begun to look paltry recently. The 14.5 percent compound total returns of the Standard & Poor's (S&P) 500 over the first six years of the 1990s has started to look very easy to people. People have begun to talk about 30 and 40 percent returns, almost as if expected. A survey of Montgomery Mutual Fund shareholders showed a 10-year expectation of a 30 percent annual growth rate! However, fear quickly takes over if the market begins to go down.

Unlike Warren Buffett or John Templeton, who treat market declines as buying opportunities, the average investor panics and throws reason to the winds. Richard Thaler's research has shown that people value a dollar lost twice as much as a dollar gained. The emotional overweighting of money lost probably accounts for a lot of the bear market panic. When people begin to lose, all kinds of fantasies are mobilized, for example, "I never should have bought any stock; people like me don't belong in the stock market; I knew this would happen; God is punishing me." These typify the ideas gripping people in a bear market.

These ideas are very consistent with psychoanalytic theory, which posits that loss is the most disorganizing event to the sense of self. Shame is one of the most powerful and primitive emotions. When people lose money, particularly if it is viewed as money that is needed, intense feelings of shame occur. A good example of this phenomenon in investing is the startling record of individual shareholders in the Magellan Fund. Between 1980 and 1992, the Magellan Fund had the astonishing record of compounded total returns of 29 percent annually. However, a controversial study attributed to Morningstar suggests that the average shareholder lost money during that period!

How could it be? Evidently it happened because the average holding period was only seven months. It appears that the average shareholder in Magellan during that period bought at a time of maximum optimism and then panicked during a minor market correction and sold. Often he or she compounded this with the kind of magical thinking that relates to guilt and loss of self-esteem. "I knew it would happen if I bought it." How many times have I heard investors say to me, "I knew when I bought it that it would go down"?

One of the greatest success stories of our time is Berkshire Hathaway. In less than 20 years, it has gone from a low of $12 a share to close at $59,000 a share on March 6, 1998. Many people have known of Warren Buffett and Berkshire but have chosen not to invest in it. For 15 years, I've been asking investors why they haven't bought Berkshire. I get two answers: one answer from the average person on the street and a different one from the professional investor. The average person says, "It costs too much." I try to explain to them that the average stock on the New York Stock Exchange sells for $35 a share. Suppose Berkshire Hathaway sells for $35,000 a share. What's the difference in having one share of Berkshire or 1,000 share of a $35 stock? They always look at me incredulously and then say, "What's the worst thing that can happen when you buy a stock? You can lose it all." I respond, "Well, you'd lose $35,000 either way."

"You don't understand," they say. "If you buy it for thirty-five thousand, you can lose all of your money, but if you buy it for thirty-five, you can save part of it." Is that logical? No it isn't. But because of Berkshire's high price, people anchor their thinking to that high number, say $35,000, and believe that is a greater risk than $35 × 1,000.

I think anybody who's ever been in retail knows that if you can't sell something, you increase your chances of selling it by increasing the price. Now you might decrease the price and have a sale. People love sales, which is another psychological problem unto itself. But if you want to move jewelry, raise the price. Car salesmen know that you should always try to start by selling people at a higher price.

The answer from professional investors as to why they haven't bought Berkshire is: "If I buy Berkshire, it's a statement to my clients that Warren Buffett is smarter than I am. How can I charge them 2 percent a year if the answer to their investing needs is to buy Berkshire Hathaway." This brings us to the issue of narcissism. Narcissism has several meanings. It has to do with loving yourself. The myth of Narcissus loving himself so much that he was punished by the gods who changed him into a flower so that he might reflect eternally upon his beauty.

Narcissism in psychoanalytic language has to do with an individual's sense of self-esteem. A degree of narcissism is necessary in order to grow to be a healthy person, that is, to have good self-esteem. So when we talk about the psychology of the self and narcissism, we're talking about a sense of self-esteem. The question of narcissism is an interesting one in investing. Everyone has heard the saying, "The stock doesn't know you own it." It's a widespread phenomenon that people do feel identified with their investments and do unconsciously think that the stock knows that they own it. David Ryan, who works for William O'Neil and *Investor's Business Daily,* talks about his first stock purchase as a child: Beechnut. He believed that every time he bought Lifesavers candy he was helping drive up its stock price. Ryan voiced a fantasy that many people have. It's very common for shareholders to buy company products with the feeling that they are contributing to a shared endeavor.

Narcissism also affects how people react to a cold call from a brokerage firm. Everyone gets these calls, but why does anyone accept them? I was very surprised a couple of years ago when I was speaking at a conference sponsored by the Cambridge Center for Behavioral Research to be told at lunch by a world-famous investor about his difficulty in dealing with those calls. I wondered why he took the calls. You know how the routine goes: "I'm Joe Smith form Robbem, Cheatem, and Blindem. I'm not calling to sell you anything. I just want to introduce myself and ask if it's okay to call if I have a good investment idea." After you say yes, he goes on to ask a series of obvious questions the answers to which are all also yes. "Would you like to make big profits? Don't you wish you had bought Merck in 1950? Would you like to double your money with little, if any, risk?" The purpose of these questions is to get you to say yes, and to make you sound stupid if you say no. The next set of questions is all about your background; and on the surface they sound reasonable and appropriate. Their real purpose is to size up how big a fish you are and to play up to your narcissism by telling you you're smart every time you say yes.

Why would this world-class investor be caught up in such a call? What could the caller possibly have to offer? Nothing. So I listened on and figured out some key things.

Many very knowledgeable investors accept these calls. They talk to the salespeople to fulfill a narcissistic need and prove to themselves that they're smarter than the salespeople, and good salespeople know how to exploit this to their advantage. Other investors are drawn in by magical thinking akin to gambling. They know that what is too good to be true *is* too good to be true. But like the infant who thinks that the world revolves around him or like the lottery ticket purchaser who's sure that her ticket is the winning one, when Joe Smith calls back, the investor usually assumes he's calling with a pretty good idea. Whether or not you act on it, it has established some credibility for him.

A few weeks later, Joe Smith calls with a very different offer: a chance to get an IPO (initial public offering) in a hot field or a secondary offering in a tiny company that sounds pretty good. At this point, Joe Smith is counting on your greed and narcissism to catch you. He's also counting on two other psychological tricks: time and the principle of reciprocation. He will create an illusion of limited time in which to act: "I've only got this many shares, and you've got to get in by tomorrow. You've got to do it now—how can you miss out on this opportunity?" This puts pressure on the customer and creates a fear of loss.

Reciprocation is the social rule that says that if someone does you a favor, you owe him one in return. This is a very powerful principle. Cialdini has written brilliantly about it in his book *Influence: The Psychology of Persuasion.* You know how reciprocation works. A friend sends you a Christmas card, so you send him one. You're invited to a party, the next party you give you invite your host. It goes on and on. Someone gives you a gift, you return the favor at the most appropriate time. But what favor had Joe Smith done? Cialdini explains this brilliantly. Reciprocation is not only the social rule about giving and getting, but it's also an important negotiating principle. If your adversary makes a concession, you're expected to do so also.

Cialdini wrote about being approached by a Boy Scout who asked him to buy a five-dollar ticket to the annual Boy Scout circus. Cialdini recognized the Boy Scouts as a pretty good group, felt a little guilty for saying no, but he didn't really want to part with five bucks and didn't want to go to the circus. So with a lot of reluctance, he said no. The Boy Scout countered with, "Well, okay, if you don't want a ticket, how about buying a candy bar for a dollar?" So Cialdini, who doesn't like chocolate, bought a candy bar.

Now whey did he do that? Well, he turned down the five-dollar request and the Scout backed off and implied if he got a dollar, he'd be happy. So Cialdini felt he had to concede then, as we all do in that situation. Joe Smith says to you, "Do you have $50,000 to invest in this wonderful opportunity?" He knows full well that very few people are willing or able to make such a purchase, but then he makes it possible for you to invest $5,000 of $10,000. Appliance and auto salespeople use this principle all the time when they lead off with their most expensive items and back off to a lower-ticket item. In behavioral finance this is called *anchoring*. Anchoring plays an important role in negotiating. If you have a business you want to sell for $10 million and you hear that somebody who is trying to buy it is going to offer you $4 million, you don't want to come in with an asking price of $10 million. You want to come in with a price of $25 million so that, as you play the game of concessions, you end up near what you want. If you begin with a starting price that is too low, you've anchored yourself at a bad spot—thus the low-ball/high-ball game.

Returning to the issue of narcissism, ownership of a stock sharply alters our perception of its value. An interesting study was done at Cornell University and the University of California. One-half of a psychology class was given a coffee mug. They were called the owners group and were asked to write down the minimum price for which they would sell their mug. The other half of the class was called the buyers group and was asked to write down the maximum price they would pay for a mug. The owners group answer averaged $5.75, and the buyers group answer averaged $2.25. When, at the end of the exercise, each group was offered the choice of either keeping a mug or receiving the price they had set, the majority of "owners" elected to keep their mugs, while the majority of the "buyers" opted for the money.

By calling them owners, by having them handle the mug, by having them write a little description of it, "owners" began to invest their own narcissism in the mugs. Therefore, they overvalued it. Meanwhile, the buyers group, first of all, hadn't gotten a mug, and they didn't like that. Secondly, they were called buyers. They didn't like that. And at the end, when the offer was made to them, they declined the mug because they had already devalued it.

Once an investor purchases a stock, his or her perception of its potential value increases substantially. The investor hears only the positive aspects of it, and tends to deny and to dismiss anything negative. This tendency is strongly enhanced if the stock rises in price, even just a little bit. On the other hand, denial sets in if the stock drops a little bit. If the stock drops a little more, the investor becomes very anxious and panics. He or she doesn't ask reasonable business questions but, instead, suffers from self-doubt—sure that he or she made a mistake and is being punished for something.

A special variation on this theme occurs among newsletter writers and stock analysts. The instant a writer or analyst talks about a stock, his or her relationship with that stock is markedly altered. Besides whatever impartial judgment existed, the writer is now burdened by having his other reputation and narcissism on the line. The wish for the stock to rise becomes a new and powerful part of the equation. This is equally true for the analysts who put themselves on the line.

We all need our heroes. Heroes are a creation of our conscience: they represent the best of ourselves, they are our idealized fathers, they help us cope with anxiety when things go wrong. If the market starts to go down and you're a value investor, say you're Warren Buffett, for example, you pull out your Ben Graham and it comforts you. Buffett himself has risen to cult status among value investors and has become the hero for the present-day generation of value investors.

There now exists a fine line between reality and unreality upon which Buffett is sitting. His teaching and preaching continues to represent Graham-esque value at its very best. The rest of the show has become an odd contradiction to the values that he has so clearly put forward. For unclear reasons, Buffett now simultaneously exploits and parodies his own image. His sophisticated life is far different than the simple, down-home, Omaha-boy image that he so carefully cultivates.

I've already exposed my psychological bias as a Freudian psychoanalyst. Now I also want to expose my investment bias as that of a value investor or, more accurately, a contrarian. Recent studies by O'Shaughnessy suggest that value-investing provides superior long-term results over any other investment philosophy. The insights of Ben Graham that advocate buying 25-cent dollar bills and the margin of safety that goes with this are the most profound market insights yet offered. The results in practice by Graham himself and his disciples, especially Buffett, John Templeton, Walter Schloss, Bill Ruane, Charlie Munger, and others, further verify this. In spite of this overwhelming evidence, the academic world of economists has long held a different view. They have espoused the Efficient Market Hypothesis, which practitioners view as partially incorrect.

Academic economists have commented on what they call an asymmetrical result. Positive earnings surprises with a high P/E group result in little market-price reaction, and positive earnings surprises with a low P/E group result in an exaggerated upside reaction. The opposite is true for a negative earnings surprise. A negative earnings surprise for the high P/E group gives a severe drop, and a negative surprise with the low P/E group doesn't result in much of a drop. I believe these results happen because the P/E multiple and other value indications are really a barometer of people's expectations of earnings. A high P/E is, in fact, a statement by Wall Street that earnings are expected to be greater than analyst forecasts, and when the earnings in fact are lower, expectations are corrected. I believe this to be a universal phenomenon and have done two studies to illustrate this.

The first study involved money. A group of people was told that they were going to get to choose from envelopes on a table. One subgroup was told that 90 percent of the envelopes had $10 and 10 percent of the envelopes had $5. They all loved this experiment. The other subgroup was told that 90 percent of the envelopes has $1 and 10 percent of them had $5.

In fact, we lied to the first subgroup: everybody was going to get $1. We lied to the second group also because everybody was going to get $10. Then we asked the entire group to rate the experiment. It was no surprise that the people who got $1 felt deceived, said this was an awful experiment, and on a rating of 0 to 10 gave an average of 2.7–a pretty "yucky" experiment! Those people who got $10 rated it nearly 8. "A wonderful experiment," said they. Somebody pointed out that there's a big difference between $1 and $10. They said that we ought to rig it so that everybody gets $5. One group is told they're going to get $10, and they actually get $5; the other group is told they're going to get $1, and they get $5, so it equalizes it.

So we did it that way and got exactly the same results. The group that was told they were going to get $10 and only got $5 rated this experiment at 2.7, unpleasant. Those who were told they were going to get $1 and got $5 rated it as an 8, a very pleasant experiment. Not very profound, right? But nevertheless, it proves the point about expectations.

Then we decided we ought to look at something that doesn't have to do with money, so we looked at pain. We took two groups of people, and we had them both do the same thing–to put their forearm up to their elbow in a bucket of ice water. This is quite painful. We measured their pulse and blood pressure every 10 seconds for 30 seconds. We told the first group in advance that this would be a pleasant experience. We said, "The water will feel cold at first, but soon you'll feel numb and it will be quite a pleasant thing." Then the other group was told "This is painful but not dangerous." Now, before we started, those told it was going to be pleasant had lower pulse and blood pressure than those told it was going to be painful.

So then when we went ahead and actually had people put their arms in the ice water. All of a sudden the people who were told it was going to be pleasant discovered it was *not* pleasant, and their pulse and blood pressure went up a lot. Meanwhile, the group told that it would be painful but not dangerous had their pulse actually drop a little bit. Their blood pressure went up some, but not a whole lot. The results were statistically significant, illustrating what I call "The Law of Unexpected Results." It is the Law of Unexpected Results that governs investor reactions to earnings surprises.

The Lexington Corporate Leaders Trust was started in 1937. Its founders decided to pick the 30 best companies in the United States for a long term equity trust. The thinking was that they were going to save a lot of money in commissions and management fees. The founders established a few simple rules for the trust. The first was that no new companies would be added. The second was that a company would be dropped from the trust only if it was acquired or went bankrupt.

Lexington Corporate Leaders Trust has been the seventh best performing mutual fund over the past decade. It has outperformed the Dow Jones Industrial Average by 3.4 percent. It has outperformed the S&P 500 throughout its existence. Why has it done that? Because of low costs. Its third rule was that when it started, instead of investing an equal dollar amount in each stock, it bought an equal *number of shares* of stock of each company. Therefore, it has a bias toward stocks that have high valuations. Another rule is that every time a stock splits, the Trust sells half of it and reinvests the proceeds equally among all the other companies so that it maintains the principle of equal numbers of shares of each stock.

My retrospective look at this, which is quite difficult to do over the period of time, indicates that while for a brief period after the split it would have been better for the Trust to have stayed in the stock, in the long run the enforced discipline and the contrarian nature requiring them to put money into what was perceived as the not-so-good stocks actually helped their performance. The last rule of the Trust is that dividends are accumulated until the Trust can buy 100 shares of every stock.

I want to summarize the essential psychological theory of contrarian investing. First, there is a fair market price for a given security, which is defined as the private market price competitors would pay for that security. Second, at times for psychological reasons, certain securities are either overvalued or undervalued. The ability to recognize these securities offers an investment advantage. Some psychological reasons for this are greed, fear, overvaluation of growth, overvaluation of newness, market mania, pessimism, and in particular the inability to predict the future.

A stock can be fairly valued on the basis of its business of the past five to seven years. It cannot be fairly valued on the basis of its business over the next five to seven years because nobody can predict it. Ben Graham had a very correct insight when he said that in the short run the market is a voting machine, but in the long run it's a weighing machine.

I will conclude with the key psychological principles that play a part in the market. One is the idea of *commitment*. When you deal with people who are resistant to following through on a financial plan, get them to put the plan in writing and to sign it or initial it. This creates a commitment that they are now much more likely to follow.

Consistency is another psychological principle that can be used to advantage for those people who have a good method and stick to it. Warren Buffett says about any investment that's brought to him, "If you don't understand it fully, I'm not interested." He has stuck to this, thereby not straying from his expertise.

Liking is another principle. People will buy from people they like. People won't fire people they like. The same is true of securities. If you like the company for whatever reason, you'll stick with it. An example of this is a widow who retains a stock because her husband loved it. Maybe the company has changed completely, but she will not sell it because she would feel that she was not being loyal to her deceased husband.

Authority is yet another guiding principle. People respond to authority. There's a very famous experiment, the Milgram Experiment, in which subjects were brought in and told to shock another subject who was behind a one-way mirror. At first, people were reluctant to administer the shock, but the more they were told to proceed and even to increase the current, the more willing they were. Social psychologists have explained this on the basis of authority and, of course, compare it to Nazi Germany.

I cautioned you in the beginning to think in many different ways. As a psychoanalyst, I believe that neither the Nazi atrocities nor the Milgram Experiment had to do with authority, except in a small way. My opinion is that both relate more significantly to our innate sadism. Every one of us has sadistic tendencies within us. Any one of us placed in such a position might do it. Why are sadistic movies so popular? Why are horror movies so popular, especially among the teenagers? Because this is material that boils within us and is given sanction to come forward. What made the results of the Milgram experiment what they were was that the authority, a superego figure, was giving people permission to act on their sadistic impulses. The people felt guilty afterward, but when they were zapping the other subjects, there is a very high likelihood that they experienced some enjoyment.

I say this because we look for ways to eliminate war but fail to recognize its role in society's sadism. We don't know how to eliminate war. We don't know how to prevent violence. Whether we ever will or not, I don't know. But we should begin by recognizing that it is inherent in all of us.

The last social/psychological principle is *scarcity*. If people think something's scarce, they feel that they have to buy it, even if it's something that they don't want. This principle also plays a role in the stock market by making hot issues so desirable. Alas, Wall Street knows this too well and responds in its own special way. It says, "When the ducks quack, feed 'em." Scarcity doesn't last long because Wall Street will bring many imitations quickly to market.

CHAPTER 6

Mindsets on Wall Street

Samuel L. Hayes, III

We are all the products of our beliefs and mindsets. I know very well that I *should* own no individual stocks, that as a small investor I am as vulnerable as a Volkswagen Rabbit on a superhighway surrounded by 18-wheelers—that is, the big, professional, institutional investors. I'm only there at the sufferance of those 18-wheelers. Instead, I should invest only in mutual funds or in professionally managed portfolios. Rationally, I shouldn't even invest in *actively* managed pools of funds. A recent *Fortune* study showed that over a 10-year period, only one in four professional managers beats the indexes. Thus, if I was really dispassionate, I would be putting my money in an index fund. But it's not much fun to come down in the morning and look at the paper and see that XYZ index fund went up or down by a piddling amount! Psychologically, I am one of those people who persists in buying stocks, even though I know I'd be better off leaving that to a professional. This is one of the contradictions we live with. Many of us never seem to lose our sense of optimism—that somehow we will prove to be the exception!

Just as psychological factors influence my actions as an individual investor, so do they influence the financial services firms on Wall Street. I have been a long-time observer of the competitive groups of vendors that operate in the financial services sector.

Psychological factors often propel these vendors in certain directions just as they do individual investors like me. I want to discuss several dimensions of that competitive behavior, and to do that I have to provide a certain amount of institutional background.

We have in the United States the best and most widely copied model of a securities industry in the world. That paradigm was originally shaped by the securities legislation of the 1930s. Since the 1930s, our financial institutions have evolved in a way somewhat different from vendors in many other countries. As a nation we have been so large, so powerful, and so self-sufficient for so long that that evolution could go forward without being substantially influenced by forces outside the country. Thus, like Darwin's species on the Galapagos Islands, we have fostered financial "animals" with certain characteristics that are of our own creation.

As a consequence of that unique evolution and of the direction that financial markets have taken in recent years, we are fortunate to have in our securities sector the preeminent wholesale investment banks in the world. They provide a creative set of value-added services and products to corporations and institutions. We also have the best-developed retail securities sector in the world. Merrill Lynch, for example, is not only a leading factor in the wholesale end of the securities business but is also the most comprehensive global retail broker.

Furthermore, we have a much-admired securities regulation model. U.S. financial markets are the world's most "transparent," which essentially means they are the most fair and the most open. Other countries, including those in the European community, are copying our model because they are persuaded that it is the best one for managing financial service activities in a very complex world. We are rapidly moving toward a global market environment wherein all countries, including the United States, must stay in sync with the dominating international financial network. There is an inevitable convergence of rules and regulations toward a model that bears a striking resemblance to that of the United States. This implies that there is less need for adaptation by U.S. participants to this global market than by vendors from other parts of the world.

Within the United States there is a continuing momentum toward deregulation, embodying the philosophy that the least regulation is the best regulation; let the markets dictate and mete out punishment where needed. However, one piece of legislation intended as a reform, the Garn-St. Germain Act in 1982, allowed the savings and loan companies to become full-fledged commercial banks and was, unfortunately, the seed for the eventual destruction of the savings and loan industry. Although there have been some other legislative initiatives, there has been no comprehensive legislative reform because special-interest lobbies have blocked it. Instead, "reform" has taken place through administrative actions that don't require legislative approval.

With these observations as background, I would like to note a couple of trends that signal contemporary mindsets on Wall Street. One is the firms' attitude toward scale and size. Another relates to a shift in priorities and loyalties of the people who work in these firms.

Large-Scale Securities Firms. The impressive growth in the size and the breadth of the leading securities firms on Wall Street is evident. For instance, in 1970, Morgan Stanley had a head count of a couple hundred people and had only one office and essentially one line of business—counseling corporations on financial market-related matters and raising money for them when needed. Today, Morgan Stanley has almost 10,000 employees, offices all over the world, and a myriad of different businesses—including a huge money management business that started from nothing in the early 1970s. In fact, Morgan Stanley is now beginning to display the outlines of a financial conglomerate.

On the retail side, there has been a consolidation to the point where there are only a handful of important national retail distribution outlets left. The two most important retail operations are, of course, Merrill Lynch and Salomon Smith Barney.

There appears to be a conviction on the part of the leadership of these wholesale and retail firms that bigger is better (and safer!). This is a significant change in attitude from a decade or two earlier. Among the "wholesale" firms who service corporations and institutional investors, it used to be an article of faith that if you stayed small and highly flexible and kept your overhead low, you had the best chance of successfully weathering an extended downturn. Now, investment banking leadership seems to value increased size of capital and breadth of products and services, apparently in an effort to smooth out cyclical patterns in individual lines of business. While this has, to some extent, produced the desired effect, it has also dramatically increased the monthly overhead "nut" that must be covered, thus heightening the importance of maintaining that steady stream of revenues and profits.

Shift in Priorities and Culture.   The way the securities firms create these profitable lines of business is to hire the very best people and then to give them plenty of room to innovate and exercise their natural entrepreneurial instincts. This has required the maintenance of at least two important conditions: (1) a highly decentralized management structure and (2) an enticing compensation scheme. As the firms have grown larger and larger, the probability of an individual making it to partner has become smaller and smaller. Individuals understood this and have been understandably unwilling to accept the traditional pattern of relatively low pay until the hallowed position of partner is achieved, at which point they get the pot of gold at the end of the rainbow! They insist on being generously paid now! And if they become dissatisfied with their arrangement with their current employer, they do not hesitate to move to another investment bank. As the partnership prospects have declined, more people are looking at their careers not as lifetime members of a partnership but as investment professionals who happened to be working for a particular firm at a particular time. The professional's objective is to maximize the psychic and material benefits that he or she can obtain from that bank, or if not that bank, some other bank. It resembles the "free agent" mentality of the baseball players and other sports figures.

The human capital (the professionals) on the one hand and the money capital (the firm's equity investors) on the other are engaged in a continuing tug-of-war over a firm's profits. The bulk of the profit pie has up to now been appropriated by the professionals.

During periods when investment banks were riding high and making record profits year after year, the firms were able to pay a large part of the pie to the professionals and still have enough left to keep the investors satisfied. But when the slowdown came in the early 1990s and the pie shrank, the professionals weren't willing to cut back their demands sufficiently to leave a reasonable return to the equity investors. That fight was played out in the public press at Salomon Brothers, where Warren Buffett tried to reconstitute the compensation arrangements so that there was a fairer split between the money capital and the human capital. He failed and had to beat a hasty retreat, but even that was not enough to prevent a number of valued professionals from walking out of Salomon for even the suggestion of such a shift in profit allocation.

Buffett's failure demonstrates the inherent difficulty that investors have in getting a fair share as owners of securities firms. The compensation arrangements provide for the professionals to take a share of earnings when the firm makes money, but not to share in losses when the firm loses money. This presents a "moral hazard" problem for the firm and its owners, whereby the professionals may be motivated to take risks that are not in the best interests of the firm's equity owners. Thus, the overall return on equity earned by the investment banking industry has not been very impressive, particularly in view of the high beta (volatility) attached to its result. It also illustrates why it has long been my belief that securities firms are best suited to be privately owned rather than publicly traded entities. Financial capital should, where possible, be supplied by the firm's own professionals rather than from public investors.

The moral hazard element is exacerbated by the decentralized structure of investment banking firms. While this structure is considered a necessary condition to provide for the entrepreneurial initiatives that have been a key to the success of these firms, it also exposes the firm to missteps by individuals or small groups of individuals. There have been some widely reported instances of this (including Baring Brothers' fall as a result of trader James Leeson's losses at their office in Singapore). In an era of decreased regulatory intervention in the day-to-day operations of the securities industry, the need for effective self-policing is magnified.

The philosophical shifts among these securities firms and individual professionals have been paralleled by a change in the mindset of Wall Street's clients. It used to be that corporate clients retained the same securities firm for many years, while the firm prospered as the customer prospered over the long term. There were occasional lucrative stipends for capital raising or mergers-and-acquisition work, and in general the vendor helped steer the client through the markets' financial shoals. That is no longer the rule, but only the exception. Corporations began some years ago to take more of their financing activities "in house," figuring that they now had the necessary capabilities and didn't need to pay an investment bank to do it for them. Further, they moved to diversify their sources of Wall Street expertise, and consequently that sense of commitment between a single investment bank and a corporate client was weakened.

A similar shift has occurred in the attitude of institutional investors. The investment banks had historically been careful to avoid conflicts of interest with their customers. But increasingly now the securities firms are acting as principals themselves, not agents, and in many cases they find themselves in competition with their own clients in trading, in arbitrage, in mergers or acquisitions, and in merchant banking and private equity. The institutional investors perceived that these firms are showing more interest in their *own* balance sheets and their own capital appreciation possibilities, rather than in ways to earn a fee from serving their clients' objectives.

In conclusion, despite the fact that the products that Wall Street buys and sells are for the most part rooted in quantitative relationships, which might suggest a set of dispassionate, numerically driven actions on the part of different parties in the financial markets, the reality is far from dispassionate. The financial markets are composed of *fallible and emotion-laden* people. Their personal priorities are and will always be an important determinant of moves in the marketplace.

CHAPTER 7

Diagnosis Before Investment

by Harry Levinson

How do you find out if a business organization is ready for the future? What assumptions do you make? What do you look for and how? How do you determine what kind of changes may be called for? And how ready is the management to make those changes? How will your approaches to these questions and answers differ from those of other investors?

These are but a few of the questions that call for *organizational diagnosis*: a comprehensive systematic effort to understand the problems, processes, behaviors, effectiveness, and adaptive success of an organization. To be adequate, let alone successful, the diagnosis must be grounded in a comprehensive understanding of human behavior. Because all science is based on theory and all theory is based on assumptions, the assumptions underlying organizational diagnosis are necessarily psychoanalytic. There are no other theories that comprehensively seek to understand unconscious, as well as conscious, motivation.

Every action by an executive, and similarly every investment decision, implies a diagnosis based on some assumptions. The major purpose of formal organizational diagnosis is to compile sufficient appropriate data to understand the organization's problems, to clarify one's assumptions by basing inferences on those data, and to interpret those data on the basis of systematic theory. Together these data enable the investor to act in a scientific way by constructing hypotheses based on data and by being able to revise those diagnostic hypotheses as necessary.

All organizations are the lengthened shadows of their founders unless there has been drastic change. The original personnel have selected successive personnel. The original accountability structure is likely to have persisted over time despite reorganizations. The set of values is likely to have been consistent over the years. In short, the investor needs to learn the organization's personality and modes of competitive adaption.

THE DIAGNOSTIC PROCEDURE

The investor should have a systematic way of gathering and organizing information. The simplest way to do this is to put the organizational diagnosis outline in my book *Organizational Diagnosis*[1] on the computer. Then, as the investor gathers information, he or she can enter those data. The investor may not want to get all of the detailed information for which the outline calls, but the general mode of getting and organizing information will be helpful.

As you begin to think of investing in an organization, your initial impressions are critical. If you visit the company, you must attune yourself to your own subtle feelings because these reflect the impact of various environmental stimuli upon you. It is helpful to ask yourself the following questions:

- What did I see in the initial contact?
- What are my initial feelings about the organization?

---

[1]Harry Levinson. *Organizational Diagnosis* (Cambridge, MA: Harvard University Press, 1972).

- What were people's attitudes toward me?
- What occurred in my visit that made me feel good, bad, or indifferent?

It is also important for you to note even vague impressions immediately as they occur. Otherwise, you will lose considerable data.

After having made contact with the organization, you begin the formal analysis. Usually this involves several steps (not necessarily in this order): (1) a breakdown of the organization to be studied into its component parts; (2) an examination of existing reports and other published data; and (3) interviews with important people outside the organization. The last may include former employees, others in the community who know the organization, competitors, suppliers, and other similarly informed people. You may not know who the relevant others are until your investigation is under way.

RELATING TO THE ORGANIZATION

A diagnostic study involves relating to an organization. An investor does not relate to an organization except as he or she relates to the people in it and particularly to the leadership.

The prospective investor will be treated in many different ways. Sometimes he or she is seen as an evaluator who judges instantaneously the innermost competencies of people or as the "unwelcome guest." He or she may be sought as the hero, the ally who is needed to give "management" or "the workers" the right point of view; or as a punisher; or as one who rewards. (These relationships often suggest the kinds of relationships people experience with one another in the organization.) The investor's approach must be one of reassurance and support. Yet, he or she may have to move into sensitive areas that are important for understanding the feelings and behavior of people.

85

FACTUAL DATA

Every organization has at least some of its policies and procedures and also various kinds of historical information on paper. Investors should become acquainted with what is on paper and develop for themselves a perspective on how it all fits together in the form of an organizational history and value system. In some instances they will be the only people who have ever thought of these data as being interrelated. Usually they will be the first to think about the collective significance of these data for the organization.

OUTSIDE INFORMATION

All organizations have relationships outside themselves—with competitors, suppliers, cooperating organizations, agents, professional associations, and so on. The investor will find it helpful to understand how the organization looks to these respective publics and should arrange, with the permission of the prospective investee, interviews with their representatives. These perspectives will enable the investor to understand how the prospective investee operates and what impact it has on others.

PATTERN OF ORGANIZATION

Almost all organizations have some form of organization chart that defines responsibilities. The investor should get one from the person who is his or her major contact but should not take the organization chart to represent the way the organization actually operates, for it may be at variance from what the organizational leadership intends. It is not unusual for working relationships to grow up informally, particularly if the organizational chart has not been published. It is important for the investor to understand why there are discrepancies and what effect they have.

INTERVIEW DATA

Depending on how significant his or her investment is likely to be, the investor should interview all of the top management group, the heads of each of the major functional groups that is being studied, and even randomly selected members of each of those functional groups.

The general tone of this approach by the investor is to invite those in the organization to help him or her understand the company. The investor should attempt to establish a collaborative relationship rather than an exploitative one. Often, resistance is mobilized because the investor is seen as a threat. However, he or she can demonstrate that his or her intention is not to get answers that will be used against top management, but to gather information as an independent professional having to make a major decision about whether to invest and how much.

The investor should precede each interview by introducing himself or herself to the interviewee, stating the purpose of the inquiry, and emphasizing its confidential nature. Even if the CEO (chief executive officer) has given a clear explanation of the investor's reason for interviewing people, most people will remain unclear about the intent. Some will have heard rumors that need to be corrected. Others may formulate rumors even if the investor is very specific about his or her intent.

When the interview is completed, the investor should permit the respondent to ask any questions he or she has to further clarify the investor's intent. Some interviewees will ask if their answers are like the replies of other respondents. This usually is a question to test the interviewer, who should reply that inasmuch as the interviews are confidential, he or she cannot disclose what other individuals have said. But sometimes the investor can offer a general response that satisfies the questioner.

OBSERVATION AND ON-THE-JOB CONTACTS

The wise investor will spend as much time as possible observing on site, asking people to explain what they do, how they do it, and what problems are inherent in getting their work done. This may involve walking from machine to machine or attending various kinds of meetings or sitting in on training and orientation programs.

There are no simple rules for initiating contact and conversation on the job. "How long have you worked here?" can provide an easy start for someone because the answer is simple and it refers to the past, which is generally less threatening than the present.

The investor should observe the different levels of comfort that people exhibit in dealing with the investor and should note how work is initiated and terminated—there may be a rush from the job at break time and heavy sighs of relief. As a supervisor passes, one may see a subordinate grit his teeth or turn to a co-worker and say something that leads the other to laugh. The investor must keep his attention sufficiently dispersed to understand interpersonal relations that occur naturally.

An investor also should look for experiences that appear stressful to people. What kinds of occurrences disrupt or disorganize people and lead them to seek help? What situations stimulate worry? While one can and should ask about these, there are many opportunities to observe them in everyday life on the job.

There are other questions that will aid in a general assessment of characteristic on-the-job experiences:

- Do people like to leave the job to talk with the investor so they can get away from it? How do they break off the interview when they are called by their supervisor?

- Do people go into some detail in explaining their jobs? Do they feel their work is a sufficiently important aspect of what goes on in the organization so that the investor should know it well?

- What aspects of the job are most gratifying? What are difficult, frustrating, or trying aspects of the job? Can and do people resolve many of these difficulties themselves? From whom do they get support and technical help?

- What other people are brought in during conversation? Which people are viewed positively and negatively and why?

- In the total context, does the person focus primarily on his or her job and the setting or on the organization as a whole? How much focus is there on the purposes served by his or her activities? Does he or she see himself or herself as a specialist with considerable skill or as doing something that anyone can do?

WORK EXPERIENCE: RATIONALE

The fact that the investor interviews someone at the worksite assures the interviewee of the investor's interest in his or her work. The investor demonstrates enough interest in what he or she can learn not only to come to the organization, but also to come "all the way" to the interviewee and that part of the company that the latter knows best.

The on-the-job interview permits the investor to observe a person reacting to his or her job situation—its demands, its uniqueness—a small sample of the total work-life experience. The investor sees what the subject's task demands, in thought and motor skills, the number and quality of interpersonal transactions, and sources of gratification and frustration. Such observations alone help the investor to learn much about those experiences that have peculiar psychological and emotional impact on the person. In turn, the investor may develop a sense of potential workforce problems that management does not recognize or is reluctant to confront.

The general questions to be kept in mind to insure coverage of key areas during the interview are:

- What are this person's sources of involvement and lack of involvement and dissatisfaction?

- How does this person's work contribute to his or her knowledge and judgment about himself or herself?
- How does he or she perceive and respond to others at work?
- What meaning does his or her activity and productivity have for him or her?
- What are normative stresses for him or her and what coping techniques does he or she utilize in dealing with them?

At the end of the interview, the investor should thank the person and should demonstrate the help he or she has given by referring to something learned from him or her. It is important to leave the interviewee with the sense having contributed. Ideally, the investor should make notes on the interview.

CASE STUDY OUTLINE

I. Genetic Data

A. Identification
The identifying information is used primarily for administrative and classification purposes. As in the lead of a newspaper report, this section contains the who, what, when, where, why, and how of the investigation. Most of the items here should be written up immediately after the initial visit to the organization.

B. History
To have meaning for the purposes of facilitating change, the description of any organization must be viewed in its historical context. The investor must know not only how the organization is functioning now, but also how those forces evolved and what historical forces continue to influence the organization's activities. However, one must strive for the truly salient points.

C. Purpose of Investigation

The data incorporated here should be verifiable. They provide the factual basis for all subsequent diagnostic hypotheses and for the conclusions that follow. They form the foundation for answering two questions: (1) How did this organization evolve? and (2) Why is it worthy of significant investment now? Therefore, as is the case with a mystery novel, this section must contain all the facts needed to substantiate the subsequent inferences.

II. Description and Analysis of Current Organization as a Whole

A. Structural data

Having identified the organization, outlined its history, and defined the purposes and conditions of the investigation, the investor now describes the organization as he or she finds it. This section is largely a factual account of how the organization is put together and how it operates. Many of the data for this section may come from formal reports and records that the organization maintains; some of it will be formulated by the investor from his or her observations and interviews.

Most organizations are put together in ad hoc fashion with no reasonable psychological logic for their form and structure. It will be particularly useful for the investor to understand Elliott Jaques's[2] conceptions on organizational structure, particularly his emphasis on accountability.

A major problem in all organizations is the degree to which individual managers and executives are able to handle the complexity of information with which they must deal. If organizations are not organized according to principles of

---

[2]Elliott Jaques. *Requisite Organization: The CEO's Guide to Creative Structure and Leadership* (Arlington, VA: Cason Hall, 1989). Elliott Jaques and Kathryn Cason. *Human Capabilities* (Arlington, VA: Cason Hall, 1994).

mental processing, as Jaques has outlined them, then there is a serious risk that many people will be misplaced, will be unable to deal with the complexity of their roles, and will lack role clarification.

B. Process data
An enormous amount of information is available to all organizations, most of which utilize only a small amount of it. The system for receiving, organizing, and integrating information is usually not clear, even to those working in the organization. However, such a process occurs whether the organization recognizes it or not. Observation and interview will quickly disclose that there is a regularity to information acquisition and information handling. The questions for the investor are: What does the organization "pick up" from its environment and what from inside itself? To what particular kinds of communication is it especially sensitive? How is what it receives transmitted inwardly? At what point is the communication interpreted, organized, assimilated, or rejected? Having accomplished that process, however inadvertently, how does the organization respond to the data it receives?

III. Interpretative Data

The data gathered prior to this point in the process have been almost wholly factual. Those inferences that have had to be made at various points were limited extrapolations from the data and could be made by most people without specialized training.

Now, however, the investor must begin to exercise his or her professional judgment. Different investors may arrive at different interpretations, depending on their training, experience, and theoretical orientation. Regardless of these factors, every investor should be aware that he or she is dealing with inference; he or she must be prepared to offer evidence for the interpretations he or she makes and the conclusions he or she reaches. Investors can indicate how well they have tested the hypothesis they advance, can specify the sources of their knowledge, and can identify speculation and opinion only by offering evidence to themselves or to others.

A. Current organizational functioning
Current organizational functioning refers to how the organization learns, thinks, feels, and behaves—roughly the equivalent of its physiology and psychology.

1. Organizational perceptions

    a. Degree of alertness, accuracy, and vividness.
    Here the investor should be concerned with the extent to which and with what effectiveness the organization recognizes and uses what is available to it. The investor must make a subjective judgment about the "degree of alertness": How alert is an organization to what is going on? How accurate and vivid are its perceptions to stimuli within the organization—from people and from its physical plant? How accurate and vivid are its perceptions to direct stimuli from outside the organization— marketing and purchasing conditions, labor conditions— and to indirect stimuli such as government influence, transportation, competition, research developments, and general economic, social, and political trends?

    b. Direction and span of attention.
    Here the investor should learn what an organization concentrates its attention on and how wide its focus is. To what stimuli does it give the most attention? In what direction is its organizational radar turned?
    All organizations concentrate selectively on some aspects of their environment. In some organizations this is formalized. Other organizations continuously concentrate on those issues that are important to the organization's leadership.
    After having interpreted what an organization pays

attention to, an investor must make a judgment about those seemingly relevant matters to which the organization is not attuned. Those things that an organization doesn't pay attention to—if they apply to its survival—will ultimately be the source of its downfall. If an organization cannot recognize relevant stimuli, this suggests impairment in organizational functioning.

c. Assessment of the discrepancy between reality and perceived reality.
The investor must now assess the organizational perceptions he or she has documented. Is there a difference between reality as the organization perceives it and as the investor sees it? An organization may be accurate in its perception of some stimuli but be incorrect in its interpretation of them. Sometimes an organization believes itself to be inept in a certain area; with new leaders, it may rise to unexpected heights. The converse is also true. Sometimes an organization precipitates its own difficulties and then must live with self-fulfilling prophecies.

2. Organizational knowledge
What body of information does the organization possess on which and with which it can act? Such information is usually transmissible in the form of techniques, history, experience, specialized competence, research data, and project reports. How an organization acquires and uses knowledge is an indication of its adaptability. Here the investor must be careful to distinguish "communication," which is a transmission of perceptions, and "internalization," that which is organized, integrated, anchored, and "owned" within the organization as one of its strengths. The task of the investor at this point is to interpret (from previously noted data) what the organization has learned and how.

Having observed, described, and interpreted how and what kinds of knowledge are acquired by whom, the investor must determine whether the information is used as an organizational asset: How is it disseminated and assimilated? Does it serve the organization? Are authority figures consciously used as models in disseminating knowledge? Is new knowledge stated in memorandum or procedure form with the assumption that people will then apply it without the need for models or instruction? Are people formally trained to use new knowledge?

3. Organizational language

Organizational language tells people what is going on in the organization. It is, therefore, important to note and to interpret the meaning of how the organization "speaks." The investor should analyze the style, content, syntax, attitudes, and values that appear in organization communications. He or she should be particularly interested in the feelings that are disguised by language used, the degree to which the organizational language is a barrier to discourse within the organization or between the organization and others, and the degree to which it constitutes a cultural or industrial boundary.

4. Emotional atmosphere

The investor needs to find out how it feels to work in the organization. The emotional atmosphere can be hectic but congenial, noisy, and joyous, or it can be loud and hostile. It may, in effect, say to people, "Be on your guard and control yourself," or "Enjoy, enjoy," or "One slip and you're out." In other words, is it pleasant and supportive? Or is it hostile and threatening?

5. Organizational action

Here the investor is concerned with how the organization acts, its characteristic style of behavior. Sometimes organizations are described as fast moving, lean and hungry, bumbling, and so on. Each of these words or phrases captures a nuance of what is meant by organizational action.

What is the pace of the organization? With what degree of enthusiasm or lethargy does it pursue new products, different markets, and innovative technology? To what extent does the organization confront problems head on? How aggressive is it in its competitive efforts? In speaking of the degree of vigor of an organization, the investor will be making a value judgment. Implicitly or overtly he or she will be comparing this organization to another. It is these subtle distinctions that allow the investor to make important judgments.

B. Attitudes and relationships

When aspects of an organization's perceptions, knowledge, language, emotional level, and modes of action are integrated, they result in its characteristic attitudes and relationships. Having made inferences from the factual data about the many ways in which the organization is functioning, the investor now must synthesize his or her inferences into statements about the organization's psychological stance.

What feelings lie behind the ways the organization functions? The focus here is on enduring psychological perspectives that provide unity, cohesion, and consistent direction to organizational behavior or, conversely, that may be detrimental to it. These are reflected in attitudes toward major dimensions of existence: attitudes toward self and others and toward time, work, and authority. It is imperative to understand attitudes and relationships because they represent methods for coping with continuing problems. Also, any attempt at intervention or change will necessarily involve an alteration in the configuration of the organization's attitudes and relationships. It is the configuration, rather than isolated variables, that must be dealt with in order to effect change.

The investor's attention should focus on which of the relations the organization has the strongest connections to and feelings about: In what things and ideas does the organization invest itself psychologically? What differences are there in investment or attachment to objects and ideas within the organization? What psychological purposes do such investments serve? (For example, it has been argued that Apple Computer Co. idealized and overinvested itself in its specific product, even addressing it as "Mac," as if it were a person. Similarly, IBM was once criticized for overpreoccupation with mainframes.) Beyond ideals, what other abstractions have meaning for the organization? What is the self-concept of the organization? How do members of the organization see themselves collectively, in relationship to other organizations and to their host community, and in their interactions and relationships?

The investor should write a brief character sketch of the key individuals. Then it is important to interpret specifically the emotional relationships among key people.

If possible, the investor should specify what he or she thinks are the most significant groups in the organization and what the relationships are between or among them. In specifying the groups he or she thinks important and delineating their relationship, the investor should look particularly into their points of difference and conflict in an effort to understand why they differ. In assessing the relationships between or among groups, the investor will want to look at how they communicate with each other, what nonwork activities they undertake together, and under what conditions they mobilize against a common outside threat. The investor's understanding of the significant groups in the organization will be crucial to his or her subsequent recommendations.

IV. Analysis and Conclusions

The conclusions at which the investor arrives at will establish a basis for his or her understanding of the affairs of the organization. Because there is no consensus on established criteria for assessing an organization, the investor's conclusions necessarily will be based on subjective interpretations.

The distillation and extraction process necessary for a useful body of conclusions is analogous to the making of fine wine. Just as the vintner selects and processes the grapes, presses them, and filters out the extraneous matter to produce wine, so the investor, from the accumulated data, must select and condense those that will reveal the essence of the organization's vitality. He or she must describe comprehensively the dynamic organizational processes, taking into account both internal and external interactions, in order to delineate and clarify the multiple determinants that bring about the organization's current adaptive behaviors. The processes that this organizational diagnostic study elicits are a reflection of the conflicts with which the organization contends in order to survive. From this study, therefore, the investor can assess the organization's various strengths and weaknesses as they enhance or interfere with the ability to cope with its marketplace and economic environment.

The question always before the investor is: How does this organization experience its strengths and problems, that is, how severe do the problems appear to be to the organization? And how well does the organization relate them to basic causes?

A. Organizational integrative patterns
As we review organizational integrative efforts, we are talking about the manner in which the organization is functioning cohesively and effectively, as well as where it is disjointed, where it fails, where it errs repetitively, and where it dissipates energy.

B. Summary and recommendations

The data the investor has gathered and interpreted have provided him or her with the material needed for viewing the organization and its external and internal environments from both a longitudinal and a cross-sectional point of view. From this dual perspective, the investor can make a definitive statement of the current status of the organization. Finally, an explanatory formulation will provide him or her with the dynamic and genetic understanding of the organization's current status. Based on perspective, current status, and explanatory formulation, the investor may formulate a prognosis: how well this organization is likely to cope with the future, in what period of time, with what necessary resources, and with what limitations.

FEEDBACK

Having completed the investigation, the investor might well feed his observations and conclusions back to the organization. This is a form of saying thanks to the CEO for opening the organization to such an evaluation and leaves the management with an appropriate closure for the experience.

When the investor is finished, he or she should review his or her notes, specify on paper for himself what he or she thinks has been learned, what mistakes have been made, and what might be done differently the next time. Unless the investor is always a learner, he or she will quickly become obsolete.

CHAPTER 8

Momentum Strategies

Louis K. C. Chan, Narasimhan Jegadeesh, and Josef Lakonishok*

An extensive body of recent finance literature documents that the cross section of stock returns is predictable based on past returns. For example, DeBondt and Thaler (1985, 1987) report that long-term past losers outperform long-term past winners over the subsequent three to five years. Jegadeesh (1990) and Lehmann (1990) find short-term return reversals. Jegadeesh and Titman (1993) add a new twist to this literature by documenting that over an intermediate horizon of three to twelve months, past winners on average continue to outperform past losers, so that there is "momentum" in stock prices.

Authors' notes: This chapter was originally published in the *Journal of Finance* 51 (no. 5), December 1996. Reprinted with permission.

*Department of Finance, College of Commerce & Business, Administrator, University of Illinois at Urbana-Champain.
We thank for their comments Mark Carhart, Eugene Fama (the referee), David Ikenberry, Prem Jain, Charles Jones, Jason Karceski, Tim Loughran, Jay Ritter, René Stulz, and an anonymous referee, as well as seminar participants at Arizona State University, 1996 Berkeley Program in Finance, the Chicago Quantitative Alliance Third Annual Conference, the Institute for International Research Conference on Behavioral Finance, the NBER Summer 1995 Institute on Asset Pricing, the Second Annual Conference on the Psychology of Investing, the University of Illinois, the University of Southern California, the University of Toronto and Yale University. We also thank Qiong Zhang for research assistance. Partial computing support was provided by the National Center for Supercomputing Applications, University of Illinois at Urbana-Champaign.

Investment strategies that exploit such momentum, by buying past winners and selling past losers, predate the scientific evidence and have been implemented by many professional investors. The popularity of this approach has grown to the extent that momentum investing constitutes a distinct, well-recognized style of investment in the United States and other equity markets.

The evidence on return predictability is, as Fama (1991) notes, among the most controversial aspects of the debate on market efficiency. Accordingly, a large number of explanations have been put forward to account for reversals in stock prices. For example, Kaul and Nimalendran (1990) and Jegadeesh and Titman (1995) examine whether bid-ask spreads can explain short-term reversals. Short-term contrarian profits may also be due to lead-lag effects between stocks (Lo and MacKinlay (1990)). De Bondt and Thaler (1985, 1987), and Chopra, Lakonishok, and Ritter (1992) point to investors' tendencies to overreact. Competing explanations for long-term reversals are based on microstructure biases that are particularly serious for low-priced stocks (Ball, Kothari, and Shanken (1995), Conrad and Kaul (1993)), or time-variation in expected returns (Ball and Kothari (1989)). Since differences across stocks in their past price performance tend to show up as differences in their book-to-market value of equity and in related measures as well, the phenomenon of long-term reversals is related to the kinds of book-to-market effects discussed by Chan, Hamao, and Lakonishok (1991), Fama and French (1992), and Lakonishok, Shleifer, and Vishny (1994).

The situation with respect to stock price momentum is very different. In contrast to the rich array of testable hypotheses concerning long- and short-term reversals, there is a woeful shortage of potential explanations for momentum. A recent article by Fama and French (1996) tries to rationalize a number of related empirical regularities, but fails to account for the profitability of the Jagadeesh and Titman (1993) strategies. In the absence of an explanation, the evidence on momentum stands out as a major unresolved puzzle. From the standpoint of investors, this state of affairs should also be a source of concern. The lack of an explanation suggests that there is a good chance that a momentum strategy will not work out-of-sample and is merely a statistical fluke.

The objective of this article is to trace the sources of the predictability of future stock returns based on past returns. It is natural to look to earnings to try to understand the movements in stock prices, so we explore this avenue to rationalize the existence of momentum. In particular, this article relates the evidence on momentum in stock prices to the evidence on the market's underreaction to earnings-related information. For instance, Latane and Jones (1979), Bernard and Thomas (1989), and Bernard, Thomas, and Wahlen (1995), among others, find that firms reporting unexpectedly high earnings outperform firms reporting unexpectedly poor earnings. The superior performance persists over a period of about six months after earnings announcements. Givoly and Lakonishok (1979) report similar sluggishness in the response of prices to revisions in analysts' forecasts of earnings. Accordingly, one possibility is that the profitability of momentum strategies is entirely due to the component of medium-horizon returns that is related to this earnings-related news. If this explanation is true, then momentum strategies will not be profitable after accounting for past innovations in earnings and earnings forecasts. Affleck-Graves and Mendenhall (1992) examine the Value Line timeliness ranking system (a proprietary model based on a combination of past earnings and price momentum, among other variables), and suggest that earnings surprises account for Value Line's ability to predict future returns.

Another possibility is that the profitability of momentum strategies stems from overreaction induced by positive feedback trading strategies of the sort discussed by DeLong, Shleifer, Summers, and Waldmann (1990). This explanation implies that "trend-chasers" reinforce movements in stock prices even in the absence of fundamental information, so that the returns for past winners and losers are (at least partly) temporary in nature. Under this explanation, we expect that past winners and losers will subsequently experience reversals in their stock prices.

Finally, it is possible that strategies based either on past returns or on earnings surprises (we refer to the latter as "earnings momentum" strategies) exploit market underreaction to different pieces of information. For example, an earnings momentum strategy may benefit from underreaction to information related to short-term earnings, while a price momentum strategy may benefit from the market's slow response to a broader set of information, including longer-term profitability. In this case we would expect that each of the momentum strategies is individually successful, and that one effect is not subsumed by the other. True economic earnings are imperfectly measured by accounting numbers, so reported earnings may be currently low even though the firm's prospects are improving. If the stock price incorporates other sources of information about future profitability, then there may be momentum in stock prices even with weak reported earnings.

In addition to relating the evidence on price momentum to that on earnings momentum, this article adds to the existing literature in several ways. We provide a comprehensive analysis of different earnings momentum strategies on a common set of data. These strategies differ with respect to how earnings surprises are measured and each adds a different perspective. In the finance literature, the most common way of measuring earnings surprises is in terms of standardized unexpected earnings, although this variable requires a model of expected earnings and hence runs the risk of specification error. In comparison, analysts' forecasts of earnings have not been as widely used in the finance literature, even though they provide a more direct measure of expectations and are available on a more timely basis. Tracking changes in analysts' forecasts is also a popular technique used by investment managers. The abnormal returns surrounding earnings announcements provide another means of objectively capturing the market's interpretation of earnings news. A particularly intriguing puzzle in this regard is that Foster, Olsen, and Shevlin (1984) find that while standardized unexpected earnings help to predict future returns, residual returns immediately around the announcement date have no such power. Our analysis helps to clear up some of these lingering issues on earnings momentum. We go on to confront the performance of price momentum with earnings momentum strategies, using portfolios formed on the basis of one-way, as well as two-way, classifications. These comparisons, and our cross-sectional regressions, help to disentangle the relative predictive power of past returns and earnings surprises for future returns. We also provide evidence on the risk-adjusted performance of the price and earnings momentum strategies.

We confirm that drifts in future returns over the next six and twelve months are predictable from a stock's prior return and from prior news about earnings. Each momentum variable has separate explanatory power for future returns, so one strategy does not subsume the other. There is little sign of subsequent reversals in returns, suggesting that positive feedback trading cannot account for the profitability of momentum strategies. If anything, the returns for companies that are ranked lowest by past earnings surprise are persistently below average in the following two to three years. Security analysts' forecasts of earnings are also slow to incorporate past earnings news, especially for firms with the worst past earnings performance. The bulk of the evidence thus points to a delayed reaction of stock prices to the information in past returns and in past earnings.

The remainder of the article is organized as follows. Section I describes the sample and our methodology. Univariate analyses of our different momentum strategies are carried out in Section II, while the results from multivariate analyses are reported in Section III. Section IV examines whether price and earnings momentum are subsequently corrected. Section V checks that our results are robust by replicating the results for larger companies only, and by controlling for risk factors. Section VI concludes.

I. SAMPLE AND METHODOLOGY

We consider all domestic, primary stocks listed on the New York (NYSE), American (AMEX), and Nasdaq stock markets. Closed-end funds, Real Estate Investment Trusts (REITs), trusts, American Depository Receipts (ADRs), and foreign stocks are excluded from the analysis. Since we require information on earnings, the sample comprises all companies with coverage on both the Center for Research in Security Prices (CRSP) and COMPUSTAT (Active and Research) files. The data for firms in this sample are supplemented, wherever available, with data on analysts' forecasts of earnings from the Lynch, Jones, and Ryan Institutional Brokers Estimate System (I/B/E/S) database.

At the beginning of every month from January 1977 to January 1993, we rank stocks on the basis of either past returns or a measure of earnings news. To be eligible, a stock need only have data available on the variable(s) used for ranking, even though we provide information on other stock attributes. The ranked stocks are then assigned to one of ten decile portfolios, where the breakpoints are based only on NYSE stocks. In our earnings momentum strategies, the breakpoints in any given month are based on all NYSE firms that have reported earnings within the prior three months. This takes into account a complete cycle of earnings announcements. All stocks are equally weighted within a given portfolio.

The ranking variable used in our price momentum strategy is a stock's past compound return, extending back six months prior to portfolio formation. In our earnings momentum strategies, we use three different measures of earnings news. Our first is the commonly used standardized unexpected earnings (SUE) variable. Foster, Olsen, and Shevlin (1984) examine different time series models for expected earnings and how the resulting measures of unanticipated earnings are associated with future returns. They find that a seasonal random walk model performs as well a more complex models, so we use it as our model of expected earnings. The SUE for stock i in month t is thus defined as

$$SUE_{it} = \frac{e_{iq-j} - e_{iq-4}}{\sigma_{it}} \tag{1}$$

where e_{iq} is quarterly earnings per share most recently announced as of month t for stock i, e_{iq-4} is earnings per share four quarters ago, and

Σ_{it} is the standard deviation of unexpected earnings, $e_{iq} - e_{iq-4}$, over the preceding eight quarters.

Another measure of earnings surprise is the cumulative abnormal stock return around the most recent announcement date of earnings up to month t, ABR, defined as

$$\text{ABR}_{it} = \sum_{j=-2}^{+1} \left(r_{it} - r_{mj} \right) \qquad (2)$$

where r_{ij} is stock i's return on day j (with the earnings being announced on day 0) and r_{mj} is the return on the equally-weighted market index. We cumulate returns until one day after the announcement date to account for the possibility of delayed stock price reaction to earnings news, particularly since our sample includes Nasdaq issues that may be less frequently traded. This return-based measure is a fairly clean measure of earnings surprise, since it does not require an explicit model for earnings expectations. However, the abnormal return around the announcement captures the change over a window of only a few days in the market's views about earnings. The SUE measure incorporates the information up to the last quarter's earnings and hence in principle measures earnings surprise over a longer period.

Our final measure of earnings news is given by changes in analysts' forecasts of earnings. Since analyst estimates are not necessarily revised every month, many of the monthly revisions take the value of zero. To get around this, we define REV6, a six-month moving average of past changes in earnings forecasts by analysts:

$$\text{REV}_{it} = \sum_{f=0}^{6} \frac{f_{it-j} - f_{it-j-1}}{P_{it-j-1}} \qquad (3)$$

where f_{it} is the consensus (mean) I/B/E/S estimate in month t of firm i's earnings for the current fiscal year (FY1). The monthly revisions in estimates are scaled by the prior month's stock price.[1] Analyst estimates are available on a monthly basis[2] and dispense with the need for a model of expected earnings. However, the estimates issued by analysts may be colored by other incentives such as the desire to encourage investors to trade and hence generate brokerage commissions.[3] As a result, analysts' forecasts may not be a clean measure of expected earnings.

For each of our momentum strategies, we report buy-and-hold returns in the periods subsequent to portfolio formation. Returns measured over contiguous intervals may be spuriously related due to bid-ask bounce, thereby attenuating the performance of the price momentum strategy. To control for this effect, we skip the first five days after portfolio formation before we begin to measure returns under the price momentum strategy and, for the sake of comparability, under the earnings momentum strategy as well. If a stock is delisted after it is included in a portfolio but before the end of the holding period over which returns are calculated, we replace its return until the end of the period with the return on a value-weighted market index.

---

[1]Scaling the revisions by the stock price penalizes stocks with high price-earnings ratios. To circumvent this possibility, we also scaled revisions by the book value per share. We also experimented with the percent change in the median I/B/E/S estimate, as well as the difference between the number of upward and downward revisions as a proportion of the number of estimates. Our results are robust to these alternative measures of analyst revisions.

[2]In the context of an implementable investment strategy, all stocks are candidates for inclusion in our price momentum or earnings momentum portfolios in a given month. The strategy based on analysts' revisions automatically fulfills this requirement, since consensus estimates are available at a monthly frequency. The portfolios based on standardized unexpected earnings and abnormal announcement returns will pick up an earnings variable that may be somewhat out-of-date for those firms not announcing earnings in the month of portfolio formation. This may lead to an understatement of the returns to these two earnings momentum strategies, but in any event we are able to compare directly the results from the price momentum and from the earnings momentum strategies.

[3]Several recent examples of these kinds of pressures on analysts are described by Michael Siconolfi in "A rare glimpse at how Wall Street covers clients," *Wall Street Journal*, July 14, 1995, and "Incredible buys: Many companies press analysts to steer clear of negative ratings," *Wall Street Journal*, July 19, 1995.

At the end of the period we rebalance all the remaining stocks in the original portfolio to equal weights in order to calculate returns in subsequent periods. In addition to returns on the portfolios, we also report two attributes of our portfolios—the book-to-market value of equity and the ratio of cash flow (earnings plus depreciation) to price—at the time of portfolio formation. Finally, we also track our three measures of earnings surprise (SUE, ABR, and REV6) at the time of portfolio formation and thereafter.

II. PRICE AND EARNINGS MOMENTUM: UNIVARIATE ANALYSIS

A. Price Momentum

We first examine the ability of each of the momentum strategies to predict future returns, and the characteristics of the momentum portfolios. To lay the groundwork, Table 8.1 reports correlations between the various measures we use to group stocks into portfolios. The

Table 8.1

Correlations between Prior Six-Month Return and Past-Earnings Surprises

Correlation coefficients are calculated over all months and over all stocks for the following variables. R6 is a stock's compound return over the prior six months. SUE is unexpected earnings (the change in the most recent past quarterly earnings per share from its value four quarters ago), scaled by the standard deviation of unexpected earnings over the past eight quarters. REV6 is a moving average of the past six months' revisions in Institutional Brokers Estimate System (I/B/E/S) median analysts' earnings forecasts relative to beginning-of-month stock price. ABR is the abnormal return relative to the equally weighted market index cumulated from two days before to one day after the most recent past announcement date of quarterly earnings. The sample includes all domestic primary firms on the New York Stock Exchange (NYSE), the American Stock Exchange (AMEX), and Nasdaq with coverage on the Center for Research in Security Prices (CRSP) and COMPUSTAT. The data extend from January 1977 to December 1993.

	R6	SUE	ABR	REV6
R6	1.000			
SUE	0.293	1.000		
ABR	0.160	0.236	1.000	
REV6	0.294	0.440	0.115	1.000

correlations are based on monthly observations pooled across all stocks. Although the variables are positively correlated with one another, the coefficients are not large. In particular, the different measures of earnings surprises are not strongly associated with each other. The highest correlation (0.440) is between standardized unexpected earnings and revisions in analyst forecasts, while the correlation between analysts' revisions and abnormal returns around earnings announcements is 0.115. The low correlations suggest that the different momentum variables are not entirely based on the same information. Rather, they capture different aspects of improvement or deterioration in a company's performance.

Panel A of Table 8.2 documents the stock price performance of portfolios formed on the basis of prior six-month returns, where portfolio 1 comprises past "losers" and portfolio 10 comprises past "winners." Subsequent to the portfolio formation date, winners outperform losers, so that by the end of twelve months there is a large difference of 15.4 percent between the returns of the winner and loser portfolios. This difference is driven by the extreme decile portfolios, however. Comparing the returns on decile portfolios 9 and 2 reveals a smaller difference of 6.3 percent.

While there is prior evidence on the profitability of price momentum strategies, we go further and provide additional characteristics of the different portfolios. In Panel B, there is a fairly close association between past return performance and the portfolios' book-to-market ratios (measured as of the portfolio formation date). The portfolio of past winners tends to include "glamour" stocks with low book-to-market ratios. Conversely, the portfolio of past losers tends to include "value" stocks with high book-to-market ratios. This is not necessarily surprising, however. Even if the different portfolios had similar book-to-market ratios at the beginning of the period, book values change very slowly over time but one portfolio rose in market value by 70 percent while the other fell by 31 percent. However, the ten portfolios display smaller differences with respect to their ratios of cash flow to price. The extreme portfolios feature low ratios of cash flow to price, but for different reasons. The portfolio of past losers

Momentum Strategies

Table 8.2

Mean Returns and Characteristics for Portfolios Classified by Prior Six-Month Return

At the beginning of every month from January 1977 to January 1993, all stocks are ranked by their compound return over the prior six months and assigned to one of ten portfolios. The assignment uses breakpoints based on New York Stock Exchange (NYSE) issues only. All stocks are equally weighted in a portfolio. The sample includes all NYSE, American Stock Exchange (AMEX), and Nasdaq domestic primary issues with coverage on the Center for Research in Security Prices (CRSP) and COMPUSTAT. Panel A reports the average past six-month return for each portfolio, and buy-and-hold returns over periods following portfolio formation (in the following six months and in the first, second, and third subsequent years). Panel B reports accounting characteristics for each portfolio: book value of common equity relative to market value, and cash flow (earnings plus depreciation) relative to market value. Panel C reports each portfolio's most recent past and subsequent values of quarterly standardized unexpected earnings (the change in quarterly earnings per share from its value four quarters ago, divided by the standard deviation of unexpected earnings over the past eight quarters). Panel D reports abnormal returns around earnings announcement dates. Abnormal returns are relative to the equally weighted market index and are cumulated from two days before to one day after the date of earnings announcement. In Panel E, averages of percentage revisions relative to the beginning-of-month stock price in monthly mean I/B/E/S estimates of current fiscal-year earnings per share are reported.

	(Low) 1	2	3	4	5	6	7	8	9	10 (High)
Panel A: Returns										
Past 6-month return	−0.308	−0.126	−0.055	0.000	0.050	0.099	0.153	0.219	0.319	0.696
Return 6 months after portfolio formation	0.061	0.086	0.093	0.096	0.102	0.104	0.105	0.111	0.120	0.149
Return first year after portfolio formation	0.143	0.185	0.198	0.208	0.214	0.222	0.223	0.235	0.248	0.297
Return second year after portfolio formation	0.205	0.201	0.205	0.206	0.208	0.208	0.204	0.208	0.207	0.199
Return third year after portfolio formation	0.194	0.196	0.197	0.196	0.199	0.202	0.205	0.201	0.208	0.206
Panel B: Characteristics										
Book-to-market ratio	1.080	1.004	0.965	0.943	0.916	0.888	0.855	0.827	0.785	0.696
Cash flow-to-price ratio	0.111	0.144	0.149	0.152	0.151	0.149	0.148	0.144	0.139	0.115
Panel C: Standardized Unexpected Earnings										
Most recent quarter	−0.879	−0.336	−0.092	0.046	0.196	0.316	0.433	0.570	0.670	0.824
Next quarter	−1.052	−0.414	−0.147	0.034	0.192	0.350	0.479	0.613	0.744	0.919

Table 8.2 *(continued)*

	(Low) 1	2	3	4	5	6	7	8	9	10	(High)
Panel D: Abnormal Return around Earnings Announcements											
Most recent announcement	−0.027	−0.013	−0.007	−0.003	0.000	0.004	0.007	0.012	0.018	0.035	
First announcement after portfolio formation	−0.011	−0.004	−0.001	0.000	0.002	0.003	0.004	0.006	0.009	0.015	
Second announcement after portfolio formation	−0.002	0.000	0.000	0.001	0.001	0.003	0.003	0.003	0.005	0.008	
Third announcement after portfolio formation	0.002	0.001	0.002	0.001	0.002	0.001	0.003	0.003	0.003	0.005	
Fourth announcement after portfolio formation	0.003	0.001	0.002	0.001	0.001	0.000	0.001	0.002	0.001	0.001	
Panel E: Revision in Analyst Forecasts (%)											
Most recent revision	−2.190	−0.576	−0.401	−0.262	−0.212	−0.127	−0.129	−0.028	−0.003	0.086	
Average over next 6 months	−2.138	−0.578	−0.368	−0.282	−0.220	−0.152	−0.117	−0.068	−0.041	0.004	
Average from months 7 to 12	−1.843	−0.555	−0.378	−0.318	−0.248	−0.206	−0.191	−0.165	−0.153	−0.180	

contains stocks with relatively depressed past earnings and cash flow, while the portfolio of past winners contains glamour stocks that have done well in the past.

The last three panels of Table 8.2 provide clues as to what may be driving price momentum. Perhaps not surprisingly, the past price performance of the portfolios is closely aligned with their past earnings performance. There is a large difference between the past winners and past losers in terms of the innovation in their past quarterly earnings (Panel C). Past abnormal announcement returns (Panel D) also rise across the momentum portfolios, with a large difference (6.2 percent) between portfolios 10 and 1. Stocks that have experienced high (low) past returns are associated with large upward (downward) past revisions in analysts' estimates (Panel E).[4]

More remarkably, the differences across the portfolios in their past earnings performance continue over the periods following portfolio formation. The spread between the SUEs of the winner and loser portfolios is actually wider in the following quarter. This may simply be a symptom of a misspecified model of expected earnings,[5] so examining the behavior of returns around earnings announcement dates provides a more direct piece of evidence. We find that the market continues to be caught by surprise at the two quarterly earnings announcements following portfolio formation, particularly for the extreme decile portfolios.[6] In particular, the abnormal return around the first subsequent announcement is higher by 2.6 percent for winner stocks compared to loser stocks. In the second announcement following portfolio formation, the abnormal return is again larger for winner stocks by 1 percent. To put this in perspective, the spread in returns between portfolios 10 and 1 is 8.8 percent in the first six months after portfolio formation. The combined difference of 3.6 percent in abnormal returns around the subsequent two announcements of quarterly earnings thus accounts for 41 percent of this spread. After two quarters, there is not much difference between the portfolios' abnormal returns around earnings announcements.

---

[4]Note that in Panel E we report statistics for monthly percentage revisions in the consensus estimates (while portfolios are formed on the basis of a six-month moving average of revisions). The presence of reporting delays in the individual estimates underlying the consensus may induce apparent persistence on a month-by-month basis, so we report average percent changes over the first and second six-month periods following portfolio formation.

[5]Fama and French (1993, 1995) argue that the statistical process for earnings changed during the 1980s. It might be suggested that this prolonged period of continuous rational surprises could account for part of the earnings surprise effects in returns. On the other hand, numerous studies document the existence of earnings surprise effects before the start of our sample period. See, for example, Givoly and Lakonishok (1979), Jones and Litzenberger (1970), and Latane and Jones (1979).

[6]Note that the average abnormal return around announcement dates is positive. This is consistent with the findings of Chari, Jagannathan, and Ofer (1988).

Panel E examines the behavior of analysts' revisions in earnings forecasts. The revisions across all the portfolios are mostly negative, a finding consistent with the notion that analysts' forecasts initially tend to be overly optimistic and are then adjusted downward over time. Such optimism may reflect the incentives faced by analysts. In particular, analysts' original estimates may be overly favorable in order to encourage investors to buy a stock and hence generate brokerage income. There are more potential buyers (all the clients of the brokerage firm) than potential sellers (who are limited to current holders of the stock, given the difficulty of short-selling). Hence an analyst is less likely to benefit from issuing a negative recommendation. An unfavorable forecast may damage relations between management and the analyst, and jeopardize other relations between management and the brokerage firm (such as underwriting and investment banking).

In the period following portfolio formation, revisions for the loser portfolio are relatively unfavorable, while those for the winner portfolio are relatively favorable. The adjustments in forecasts are especially protracted for the loser portfolio, as there is a large downward monthly revision averaging 2.1 percent (relative to the stock price at the beginning of the month) in the first six months after portfolio formation. The average monthly revision from seven to twelve months afterward is still large (1.8 percent). Klein (1990) also finds that analysts remain overly optimistic in their forecasts for firms that have experienced poor stock price performance. One conjecture is that it may not be in an analyst's best interest to be the first messenger with bad news (a negative forecast), as this might antagonize management. Instead analysts may remain optimistic and wait for additional confirmatory evidence of poor earnings before slowly modifying their estimates. Further, the dependence of analysts' incomes on the amount of business they generate (as reflected by trading volume) may make them less willing to disseminate unfavorable news (see Lakonishok and Smidt (1986)). The market, however, is not necessarily taken in by such reticence on the part of analysts. The abnormal returns around earnings announcements (Panel D) show no marked asymmetries between the loser and winner portfolios and they also appear to adjust faster, so that the average abnormal return is very close to zero by the time of the third announcement following portfolio formation. All in all, the association between prior returns and prior earnings news, as well as the sluggishness in the market's response to past earnings surprises, instills some confidence that the momentum in stock prices may at least partially reflect the market's slow adjustment to the information in earnings.

B. Earnings Momentum

Investment rules based on standardized unexpected earnings (SUE) have a long history dating back at least to Jones and Litzenberger (1970) and Latane and Jones (1979). Accordingly, Table 8.3 starts off our evaluation of earnings momentum by applying a strategy based on SUE as a measure of the news in earnings. In the first six months after portfolio formation, the arbitrage portfolio (portfolio 10 minus portfolio 1) earns a return of 6.8 percent. The superior performance is relatively short-lived, however. The spread in returns after a year is only slightly higher at 7.5 percent.

The evidence in the other panels of Table 8.3 is consistent with the idea that the superior stock price performance reflects the market's gradual adjustment to earnings surprises. In particular, the past SUE contains information that is not incorporated into the stock price. Instead, at the next announcement date of earnings the market is still surprised by stocks with good or bad past SUE, and there is a difference in returns of 2.4 percent between stocks with the best and worst past SUE. At the second subsequent announcement of earnings, the abnormal returns still differ by 0.8 percent, so that almost half, or 3.2 percent, of the spread in the first six months occurs around the release of earnings. As is the case in Panel A, the higher returns do not persist for long, and by the third announcement the returns of the different portfolios are very similar. In the period following portfolio formation, the behavior of subsequent standardized unexpected earnings and consensus estimates also

115

Table 8.3

Mean Returns and Characteristics for Portfolios Classified by Standardized Unexpected Earnings

At the beginning of every month from January 1977 to January 1993, all stocks are ranked by their most recent past standardized unexpected earnings and assigned to one of ten portfolios. Standardized unexpected earnings is unexpected earnings (the change in quarterly earnings per share from its value four quarters ago) divided by the standard deviation of unexpected earnings over the past eight quarters. The assignment uses breakpoints based on New York Stock Exchange (NYSE) issues only. All stocks are equally weighted in a portfolio. The sample includes all NYSE, American Stock Exchange (AMEX), and Nasdaq domestic primary issues with coverage on the Center for Research in Security Prices (CRSP) and COMPUSTAT. Panel A reports the average past six-month return for each portfolio, and buy-and-hold returns over periods following portfolio formation (in the following six months and in the first, second, and third subsequent years). Panel B reports accounting characteristics for each portfolio: book value of common equity relative to market value, and cash flow (earnings plus depreciation) relative to market value. Panel C reports each portfolio's most recent past and subsequent values of quarterly standardized unexpected earnings. Panel D reports abnormal returns around earnings announcement dates. Abnormal returns are relative to the equally-weighted market index and are cumulated from two days before to one day after the date of earnings announcement. In Panel E, averages of percentage revisions relative to the beginning-of-month stock price in monthly mean I/B/E/S estimates of current fiscal-year earnings per share are reported.

	(Low) 1	2	3	4	5	6	7	8	9	10	(High)
Panel A: Returns											
Past 6-month return	−0.052	−0.004	−0.027	0.062	0.099	0.127	0.149	0.166	0.186	0.226	
Return 6 months after portfolio formation	0.051	0.063	0.081	0.091	0.105	0.114	0.114	0.115	0.119	0.119	
Return first year after portfolio formation	0.138	0.160	0.193	0.205	0.225	0.232	0.227	0.226	0.225	0.213	
Return second year after portfolio formation	0.169	0.183	0.194	0.212	0.218	0.215	0.218	0.211	0.204	0.180	
Return third year after portfolio formation	0.185	0.189	0.204	0.216	0.208	0.211	0.211	0.208	0.197	0.179	
Panel B: Characteristics											
Book-to-market ratio	1.074	1.046	1.028	0.995	0.935	0.894	0.834	0.802	0.759	0.700	
Cash flow-to-price ratio	0.134	0.146	0.148	0.144	0.143	0.142	0.139	0.139	0.136	0.134	

116

Table 8.3 *(continued)*

	(Low) 1	2	3	4	5	6	7	8	9	10	(High)
Panel C: Standardized Unexpected Earnings											
Most recent quarter	−2.882	−0.896	−0.398	−0.112	0.120	0.342	0.601	0.938	1.448	2.839	
Next quarter	−2.364	−0.830	−0.377	−0.083	0.125	0.356	0.589	0.839	1.219	2.282	
Panel D: Abnormal Return around Earnings Announcements											
Most recent announcement	−0.023	−0.015	−0.009	−0.004	0.003	0.008	0.012	0.015	0.017	0.022	
First announcement after portfolio formation	−0.012	−0.008	−0.005	−0.001	0.003	0.005	0.007	0.008	0.011	0.012	
Second announcement after portfolio formation	−0.003	−0.002	0.001	0.001	0.004	0.004	0.004	0.003	0.003	0.005	
Third announcement after portfolio formation	0.002	0.001	0.003	0.003	0.002	0.003	0.002	0.001	0.001	0.001	
Fourth announcement after portfolio formation	0.003	0.005	0.002	0.001	0.002	0.001	−0.001	−0.001	0.001	−0.002	
Panel E: Revision in Analyst Forecasts (%)											
Most recent revision	−1.558	−0.903	−0.547	−0.626	−0.268	−0.125	−0.059	−0.171	−0.066	0.107	
Average over next 6 months	−1.480	−0.866	−0.647	−0.453	−0.325	−0.198	−0.119	−0.095	−0.054	0.005	
Average from months 7 to 12	−1.160	−0.817	−0.659	−0.352	−0.352	−0.247	−0.296	−0.232	−0.199	−0.155	

shows delays in the adjustment of forecasts. The sustained nature of the adjustment in analysts' forecasts is particularly notable in the case of firms in portfolio 1 with large unexpected declines in earnings.

It is possible that the results in Table 8.3 are influenced by measurement errors in earnings or misspecification of the model for

117

expected earnings. Another variable that may give a clearer, more objective measure of the informativeness of earnings for investors is the stock market's response around the time when earnings are announced. Hence, Table 8.4 provides results for portfolios formed on the basis of abnormal returns around the most recent past earnings announcement. To the extent that the market responds slowly to the news in earnings, we should expect to see a drift in future stock returns that can be predicted by the sign and magnitude of the abnormal announcement return. Surprisingly, however, Foster, Olsen, and Shevlin (1984) find that future returns are associated with past SUE but not with past abnormal announcement returns. Our results in Table 8.4 actually indicate that the differences in returns associated with differences in past abnormal announcement returns are as large as the differences induced by ranking on SUE.[7] Stocks with large favorable announcement returns subsequently outperform stocks with large unfavorable announcement returns by 5.9 percent in the first six months, and by 8.3 percent in the first year. Tables 8.3 and 8.4 both suggest that the underreaction to quarterly earnings surprises seems to be a more short-lived phenomenon than the underreaction to past returns.

The news reflected in the past earnings announcement return continues to leave its traces at the next announcement following portfolio formation (Panel D). The spread in returns between stocks that have delivered favorable surprises and those with unfavorable surprises is especially striking (8.8 percent). Market forecasts of earnings, as represented by SUE or analysts' estimates, also respond slowly to the new information in announcement returns.

While behavioral or sociological considerations may impart a bias to analysts' forecasts, an upward or downward revision in the

---

[7]Bernard, Thomas, and Wahlen (1995) find, as we do, the announcement period returns help to predict future excess returns. They argue that the holding period used in Foster, Olsen, and Shevlin (1984) to track returns after an earnings announcement stops short of the next announcement. Hence, a possible explanation for the weaker results in Foster, Olsen, and Shevlin (1984) is that they miss much of the stock price reaction around subsequent announcements.

Momentum Strategies

Table 8.4

Mean Returns and Characteristics for Portfolios Classified by Abnormal Return around Earnings Announcements

At the beginning of every month from January 1977 to January 1993, all stocks are ranked by their abnormal return around the most recent past announcement of quarterly earnings and assigned to one of ten portfolios. Abnormal returns are relative to the equally weighted market index and are cumulated from two days before to one day after the date of earnings announcement. The assignment uses breakpoints based on New York Stock Exchange (NYSE) issues only. All stocks are equally weighted in a portfolio. The sample includes all NYSE, American Stock Exchange (AMEX), and Nasdaq domestic primary issues with coverage on the Center for Research in Security Prices (CRSP) and COMPUSTAT. Panel A reports the average past six-month return for each portfolio, and buy-and-hold returns over periods following portfolio formation (in the following six months and in the first, second, and third subsequent years). Panel B reports accounting characteristics for each portfolio: book value of common equity relative to market value, and cash flow (earnings plus depreciation) relative to market value. Panel C reports each portfolio's most recent past and subsequent values of quarterly standardized unexpected earnings (the change in quarterly earnings per share from its value four quarters ago, divided by the standard deviation of unexpected earnings over the past eight quarters). Panel D reports abnormal returns around earnings announcement dates. In Panel E, averages of percentage revisions relative to the beginning-of-month stock price in monthly mean I/B/E/S estimates of current fiscal-year earnings per share are reported.

(Low)	1	2	3	4	5	6	7	8	9	10	(High)
					Panel A: Returns						
Past 6-month return	−0.026	0.039	0.061	0.074	0.085	0.099	0.113	0.132	0.161	0.223	
Return 6 months after portfolio formation	0.063	0.077	0.088	0.093	0.094	0.099	0.099	0.101	0.111	0.122	
Return first year after portfolio formation	0.155	0.174	0.083	0.194	0.198	0.208	0.208	0.212	0.221	0.238	
Return second year after portfolio formation	0.186	0.190	0.185	0.192	0.197	0.198	0.199	0.196	0.205	0.207	
Return third year after portfolio formation	0.183	0.188	0.185	0.190	0.196	0.200	0.198	0.198	0.198	0.214	
					Panel B: Characteristics						
Book-to-market ratio	0.968	0.923	0.903	0.907	0.900	0.891	0.880	0.870	0.857	0.894	
Cash flow-to-price ratio	0.119	0.140	0.146	0.150	0.148	0.149	0.148	0.146	0.139	0.122	
					Panel C: Standardized Unexpected Earnings						
Most recent quarter	−0.485	−0.169	−0.005	0.126	0.191	0.273	0.329	0.364	0.465	0.508	

119

Table 8.4 *(continued)*

	(Low) 1	2	3	4	5	6	7	8	9	10	(High)
Next quarter	−0.635	−0.186	−0.034	0.119	0.183	0.256	0.293	0.371	0.499	0.529	

Panel D: Abnormal Return around Earnings Announcements

	(Low) 1	2	3	4	5	6	7	8	9	10	(High)
Most recent announcement	−0.076	−0.033	−0.020	−0.011	−0.004	0.004	0.011	0.021	0.035	0.089	
First announcement after portfolio formation	−0.040	−0.017	−0.010	−0.006	−0.001	0.003	0.007	0.012	0.020	0.048	
Second announcement after portfolio formation	−0.001	−0.002	0.000	0.001	0.002	0.002	0.003	0.003	0.004	0.007	
Third announcement after portfolio formation	0.000	0.002	0.002	0.001	0.001	0.002	0.002	0.002	0.003	0.005	
Fourth announcement after portfolio formation	0.001	0.001	0.000	0.002	0.000	0.002	−0.001	0.002	0.003	0.001	

Panel E: Revision in Analyst Forecasts (%)

	(Low) 1	2	3	4	5	6	7	8	9	10	(High)
Most recent revision	−1.135	−0.564	−0.372	−0.257	−0.261	−0.232	−0.273	−0.252	−0.338	−0.321	
Average over next 6 months	−1.314	−0.514	−0.329	−0.284	−0.263	−0.223	−0.202	−0.234	−0.312	−0.319	
Average from months 7 to 12	−1.215	−0.506	−0.363	−0.271	−0.307	−0.271	−0.280	−0.260	−0.275	−0.518	

consensus estimate may still convey information. Table 8.5 suggests that this is indeed the case. Moreover, of the three measures of earnings surprise, sorting stocks on REV6 yields the largest spread in one-year returns (9.7 percent).[8] In other respects, the results in Table 8.5 are very similar to those for either standardized unexpected earnings or announcement returns.

---

[8]We obtain similar results when we use monthly revisions in analysts' forecasts instead of a six-month moving average. Womack (1996) also finds that changes in analysts' buy or sell recommendations predict future returns.

Table 8.5

Mean Returns and Characteristics for Portfolios Classified by Revision in Analyst Forecasts

At the beginning of every month from January 1977 to January 1993, all stocks are ranked by their moving average of the past six months' revisions in mean I/B/E/S estimates of current fiscal-year earnings per share, relative to beginning-of-month stock price, and assigned to one of ten portfolios. The assignment uses breakpoints based on New York Stock Exchange (NYSE) issues only. All stocks are equally weighted in a portfolio. The sample includes all NYSE, American Stock Exchange (AMEX), and Nasdaq domestic primary issues with coverage on the Center for Research in Security Prices (CRSP) and COMPUSTAT. Panel A reports the average past six-month return for each portfolio, and buy-and-hold returns over periods following portfolio formation (in the following six months and in the first, second, and third subsequent years). Panel B reports accounting characteristics for each portfolio: book value of common equity relative to market value, and cash flow (earnings plus depreciation) relative to market value. Panel C reports each portfolio's most recent past and subsequent values of quarterly standardized unexpected earnings (the change in quarterly earnings per share from its value four quarters ago, divided by the standard deviation of unexpected earnings over the past eight quarters). Panel D reports abnormal returns around earnings announcement dates. Abnormal returns are relative to the equally weighted market index and are cumulated from two days before to one day after the date of earnings announcement. In Panel E, averages of percentage revisions relative to the beginning-of-month stock price in monthly mean I/B/E/S estimates of current fiscal-year earnings per share are reported.

	(Low) 1	2	3	4	5	6	7	8	9	10	(High)
Panel A: Returns											
Past 6-month return	−0.066	0.002	0.032	0.058	0.083	0.099	0.116	0.156	0.191	0.248	
Return 6 months after portfolio formation	0.046	0.070	0.072	0.079	0.083	0.082	0.087	0.106	0.116	0.123	
Return first year after portfolio formation	0.132	0.159	0.164	0.171	0.177	0.174	0.177	0.203	0.216	0.229	
Return second year after portfolio formation	0.159	0.180	0.178	0.187	0.180	0.171	0.178	0.175	0.188	0.214	
Return third year after portfolio formation	0.177	0.182	0.174	0.173	0.186	0.179	0.176	0.189	0.194	0.202	
Panel B: Characteristics											
Book-to-market ratio	1.232	0.986	0.877	0.803	0.740	0.681	0.669	0.694	0.752	0.881	
Cash flow-to-price ratio	0.093	0.152	0.156	0.151	0.146	0.132	0.131	0.141	0.155	0.165	

Table 8.5 *(continued)*

	(Low)	1	2	3	4	5	6	7	8	9	10	(High)
		Panel C: Standardized Unexpected Earnings										
Most recent quarter		−1.507	−0.809	−0.383	−0.036	0.323	0.566	0.855	1.014	1.155	1.122	
Next quarter		−1.098	−0.721	−0.342	−0.030	0.213	0.507	0.792	0.878	0.950	0.889	
		Panel D: Abnormal Return around Earnings Announcements										
Most recent announcement		−0.017	−0.010	−0.007	−0.004	−0.001	0.002	0.003	0.007	0.012	0.021	
First announcement after portfolio formation		−0.006	−0.004	−0.002	−0.001	−0.001	0.000	0.002	0.003	0.005	0.009	
Second announcement after portfolio formation		−0.002	0.000	0.000	0.000	−0.001	0.002	0.002	0.001	0.003	0.004	
Third announcement after portfolio formation		0.003	0.000	0.000	0.003	0.000	0.000	0.000	0.003	0.000	0.000	
Fourth announcement after portfolio formation		0.002	0.002	0.001	0.000	−0.002	0.001	0.000	0.000	0.000	−0.001	
		Panel E: Revision in Analyst Forecasts (%)										
Most recent revision		−3.453	−0.540	−0.275	−0.156	−0.073	−0.027	0.011	0.050	0.126	0.813	
Average over next 6 months		−2.027	−0.529	−0.323	−0.231	−0.158	−0.158	−0.116	−0.057	−0.037	−0.321	
Average from months 7 to 12		−1.994	−0.516	−0.320	−0.237	−0.190	−0.181	−0.153	−0.135	−0.156	−0.332	

To summarize, sorting stocks on the basis of past returns yields large differences in subsequent returns. Sorting on past earnings surprise (measured in a number of ways) also gives rise to large spreads in future returns. The spreads in returns associated with the earnings momentum strategies, however, tend to be smaller and persist for a shorter period of time when compared to the results of the price momentum strategy. Our evidence is consistent with the idea that the market does not incorporate the news in past prices or earnings promptly. Instead, the adjustment is gradual, so that there are drifts in subsequent returns. In the same manner, security analysts are slow to revise their expectations about earnings, particularly when the news in earnings is unfavorable. The asymmetry in the behavior of revisions with respect to past losers and past winners hints at the importance of the incentive structures analysts face when they issue forecasts.

III. PRICE AND EARNINGS MOMENTUM: MULTIVARIATE ANALYSIS

The evidence in Section II indicates that each of the momentum strategies that we consider is by itself useful in predicting future stock returns. We now examine whether the continuation in past price movements and the underreaction to earnings news are the same phenomenon.

A. Two-way Analysis of Price and Earnings Momentum

Our first set of tests addresses this issue in terms of a two-way classification. At the beginning of each month, we sort the securities in the sample on the basis of their past six-month returns and assign them to one of three equally sized portfolios. Independently, we sort stocks and group them into three equally sized portfolios on the basis of the most recent earnings surprise. Under this procedure each stock is assigned to one of nine portfolios. Table 8.6 reports buy-and-hold returns over each of several periods following portfolio formation, as well as the average earnings surprise over the first subsequent year. Panel A reports the results when earnings surprises are measured as abnormal returns around earnings announcements, while Panels B and C provide results for standardized unexpected earnings and analyst revisions, respectively.

Table 8.6

Postformation Returns and Earnings Surprises for Portfolios Ranked by 2-Way Classifications

In Panels A to C, at the beginning of every month from January 1977 to January 1993, all stocks are ranked by their compound return over the prior six months and assigned to one of three equal sized portfolios. All stocks are also independently ranked by a measure of earnings surprise and assigned to one of three equally sized portfolios. The assignments use breakpoints based on New York Stock Exchange (NYSE) issues only. The intersections of the sort by prior return and the sort by earnings surprise give three sets of nine portfolios each. All stocks are equally weighted in a portfolio. The sample includes all NYSE, American Stock Exchange (AMEX), and Nasdaq domestic primary issues with coverage on the Center for Research in Security Prices (CRSP) and COMPUSTAT. In Panel A, earnings surprise is measured as the abnormal return relative to the equally weighted market index, cumulated from two days before to one day after the date of the most recent past earnings announcement. In Panel B, earnings surprise is measured as the most recent past unexpected earnings (the change in quarterly earnings per share from its value four quarters ago) divided by the standard deviation of unexpected earnings over the past eight quarters. In Panel C, earnings surprise is a moving average of the past six months' revisions in mean I/B/E/S estimates of current fiscal-year earnings per share, relative to the beginning-of-month stock price. In Panels D and E, the independent rankings are by revisions in analysts' forecasts and by either past standardized unexpected earnings or by abnormal return around past earnings announcement. For each portfolio, the table shows the average buy-and-hold returns for the first six months and the first through third years following portfolio formation. Means are also given for the cumulative abnormal return around the first four announcements of quarterly earnings after portfolio formation, the first four quarterly standardized unexpected earnings after portfolio information, and percentage revisions relative to the beginning-of-month stock price in monthly mean I/B/E/S estimates of current fiscal-year earnings per share.

Panel A: Abnormal Return around Earnings Announcement and Prior 6-Month Return

Abnormal Announcement Return	1 (Low)	1	1	2	2	2	3	3	3 (High)
Prior 6-Month Return	1 (Low)	1	1	2	2	2	3	3	3 (High)
First six months	0.056	0.077	0.079	0.086	0.098	0.111	0.100	0.115	0.135
First year	0.138	0.165	0.159	0.190	0.205	0.225	0.213	0.237	0.270
Second year	0.185	0.194	0.199	0.192	0.199	0.213	0.183	0.199	0.199
Third year	0.179	0.187	0.196	0.194	0.196	0.207	0.188	0.205	0.204
Average return around next 4 earnings announcements	−0.008	0.000	0.009	−0.004	0.001	0.008	−0.003	0.003	0.012
Average of next 4 standardized unexpected earnings	−0.494	−0.251	−0.191	0.040	0.265	0.302	0.359	0.598	0.651
Average of next 12 revisions in analyst forecasts	−1.319	−0.599	−0.967	−0.306	−0.168	−0.203	−0.180	−0.078	−0.067

Table 8.6 *(continued)*

	Panel B: Standardized Unexpected Earnings and Prior 6-Month Return								
Standardized Unexpected Earnings	1 (Low)	2	3	1	2	3	1	2	3 (High)
Prior 6-Month Return	1 (Low)	1	1	2	2	2	3	3	3 (High)
First six months	0.055	0.094	0.085	0.076	0.106	0.113	0.074	0.118	0.136
First year	0.142	0.190	0.157	0.183	0.224	0.216	0.190	0.253	0.257
Second year	0.178	0.212	0.199	0.188	0.219	0.200	0.181	0.213	0.199
Third year	0.188	0.202	0.184	0.190	0.214	0.196	0.207	0.216	0.200
Average return around next 4 earnings announcements	−0.003	0.001	0.000	−0.001	0.002	0.003	0.002	0.006	0.006
Average of next 4 standardized unexpected earnings	−0.731	−0.103	0.257	−0.293	0.182	0..763	−0.090	0.385	1.048
Average of next 12 revisions in analyst forecasts	−1.549	−0.645	−0.457	−0.380	−0.184	−0.092	−0.294	−0.096	−0.013
	Panel C: Revision in Analyst Forecasts and Prior 6-Month Return								
Revision in Analyst Forecasts	1 (Low)	2	3	1	2	3	1	2	3 (High)
Prior 6-Month Return	1 (Low)	1	1	2	2	2	3	3	3 (High)
First six months	0.042	0.063	0.085	0.077	0.088	0.112	0.093	0.103	0.130
First year	0.113	0.134	0.152	0.180	0.186	0.214	0.214	0.215	0.246
Second year	0.169	0.178	0.184	0.181	0.189	0.202	0.614	0.179	0.192
Third year	0.164	0.174	0.182	0.187	0.188	0.198	0.202	0.184	0.198
Average return around next 4 earnings announcements	−0.003	−0.002	−0.003	−0.001	0.000	0.002	0.005	0.003	0.004
Average of next 4 standardized unexpected earnings	−0.589	−0.189	−0.057	−0.090	0.316	0..448	0.236	0.607	0.843
Average of next 12 revisions in analyst forecasts	−1.526	−0.376	−0.753	−0.440	−0.135	−0.130	−0.297	−0.07	−0.031

Table 8.6 *(continued)*

Panel D: Revision in Analyst Forecasts and Standardized Unexpected Earnings

Revision in Analyst Forecasts	1 (Low)	2	3	1	2	3	1	2	3 (High)
Standardized Unexpected Earnings	1 (Low)	1	1	2	2	2	3	3	3 (High)
First six months	0.051	0.065	0.093	0.084	0.093	0.111	0.093	0.096	0.121
First year	0.137	0.153	0.190	0.184	0.196	0.224	0.185	0.187	0.220
Second year	0.161	0.185	0.194	0.193	0.205	0.208	0.190	0.178	0.192
Third year	0.173	0.185	0.185	0.187	0.207	0.216	0.195	0.178	0.189
Average return around next 4 earnings announcements	−0.003	−0.001	−0.001	0.002	0.001	0.002	0.002	0.001	0.004
Average of next 4 standardized unexpected earnings	−0.618	−0.348	0.281	−0.023	0.189	0.256	−0.345	0.812	0.995
Average of next 12 revisions in analyst forecasts	−1.281	−0.302	−0.672	−0.622	−0.157	−0.180	−0.519	−0.085	−0.064

Panel E: Revision in Analyst Forecasts and Abnormal Return around Earnings Announcement

First six months	0.048	0.067	0.097	0.070	0.086	0.113	0.071	0.096	0.126
First year	0.128	0.153	0.189	0.163	0.183	0.214	0.166	0.192	0.237
Second year	0.165	0.176	0.184	0.178	0.186	0.195	0.175	0.188	0.200
Third year	0.170	0180	0.176	0.175	0.188	0.200	0.191	0.185	0.200
Average return around next 4 earnings announcements	−0.007	−0.005	−0.006	0.000	0.000	0.001	0.008	0.007	0.008
Average of next 4 standardized unexpected earnings	−0.503	0.010	0.316	−0.228	0.310	0.544	−0.099	0.418	0.691
Average of next 12 revisions in analyst forecasts	−1.366	−0.271	−0.359	−0.612	−0.136	−0.099	−0.796	−0.144	−0.140

126

The first three panels in Table 8.6 tell a consistent story. Most important, past realizations of six-month returns and earnings news predict continued drifts in returns in the subsequent period. In particular, the two-way sort generates large differences in returns between stocks that are jointly ranked highest and stocks jointly ranked lowest. For example, using past return in conjunction with earnings surprise measured as the abnormal announcement return, the highest-ranking portfolio outperforms the lowest-ranked portfolio by 7.9 percent in the first six months. Similarly, the six-month spread is 8.1 percent using prior return together with SUE, and 8.8 percent using prior return with analysts' revisions.

Each variable (prior return or earnings surprise) contributes some incremental predictive power for future returns, given the other variable. In Panel A, holding prior return fixed, stocks with high past announcement return earn in the first six months following portfolio formation 2.8 percent more on average than stocks with low past announcement return.[9] In comparison, the returns on stocks with high and low past prior return, but similar levels of announcement return, differ on average by 4.6 percent. Using measures of longer-term earnings news, as given by either standardized unexpected earnings or revisions in consensus estimates, turns out to place earnings momentum on a more equal footing with price momentum. The six-month spreads induced by past SUE or past revision, conditional on prior return, are 4.3 percent and 3.8 percent, respectively. Sorting on past return, conditional on past earnings news, produces average spreads in six-month returns of 3.1 percent (Panel B) and 4.5 percent (Panel C). The bottom line is that although the ranking by prior return generally gives rise to larger differences in future returns, neither momentum strategy subsumes the other. Instead, they each exploit underreaction to different pieces of information.

As in the earlier tables, however, there are signs in Table 8.6 that the component of superior performance associated with earnings

---

[9]In each of the three categories of prior return, we take the difference in returns between portfolios 3 and 1 when stocks are ranked by prior announcement return. The reported number is the simple mean of the three differences.

surprise is more short-lived than the component associated with prior return. As shown in Panel A, ranking stocks by past announcement return, conditional on prior return, generates average spreads in returns of 2.8 percent during the first six months and spreads of 3.8 percent in the first year. On the other hand, the sort by prior return, holding announcement return fixed, produces average spreads of 4.6 and 8.6 percent over six and twelve months, respectively. The corresponding average spreads in Panel B using sorts by SUE are 4.3 percent (3.8 percent) for six months (one year), and using sorts by prior return are 3.1 percent (7.0 percent). Similarly, sorts in Panel C using REV6 give spreads of 3.8 percent (3.5 percent for six months (one year), while sorts by prior return give spreads of 4.5 percent (9.2 percent). Apparently, the component of prior return not associated with earnings news is associated with more persistent drifts in future returns.

One possible explanation for the larger return spreads associated with price momentum, compared with earnings momentum, is as follows. Our earnings momentum strategies are based on the performance of near-term income: the innovations in quarterly earnings, or analysts' forecasts of earnings for the current fiscal year. In comparison, when we select a stock on the basis of high or low prior returns, we isolate cases where the market has made very large revisions in its expectations of the firm's future outlook. Table 8.2 confirms that the highest-ranked portfolio in our price momentum strategy rose in price by roughly 70 percent on average, while the lowest-ranked portfolio fell in price by about 30 percent on average, over the previous six months. It is unlikely that changes of this magnitude arise solely from quarter-to-quarter news in earnings. The corresponding past six-month returns of the portfolio ranked highest (lowest) by analysts' revisions, for example, is about 25 percent (–7 percent). Since there has been a larger reappraisal of market beliefs for the price momentum portfolios, and given that the markets' adjustment is not immediate, it is perhaps not surprising that the spread in future returns continues to be larger for the price momentum strategy.

In a similar vein, the difference in the persistence of the two strategies has some intuitive basis. The uncertainty underlying the short-horizon measures of profitability used in the earnings momentum strategies is resolved relatively quickly. Prior returns, on the other hand, reflect a broad set of market expectations not limited to near-term profitability. On this basis, we conjecture that it may take longer for the new information to be played out in stock prices for the price momentum strategy.

Panels D and E pit our measures of earnings surprise against each other. In general, each measure of surprise has incremental predictive power for returns and they give rise to similar spreads in average returns. Holding SUE fixed, for example, portfolios sorted by analysts' revisions generate average spreads in six-month returns of 3.23 percent; classifying by SUE while holding fixed analysts' revisions yields average spreads of 3.37 percent in six-month returns. Similarly, in Panel E, the sorts by REV6 and ABR yield average spreads of 4.90 and 2.70 percent, respectively, in six-month returns. No single measure of the news in earnings wins the contest; instead, they each add separate pieces of information, as noted in our introduction.

B. Cross-Sectional Regressions

We use Fama-MacBeth (1973) cross-sectional regressions as another way to disentangle price and earnings momentum. Every month, we fit a cross-sectional regression of individual stock returns on the prior six-month return and various measures of the most recent past earnings surprise (SUE, ABR, and REV6). We also include firm size as a catchall variable for other influences on the cross section of returns. To account for possible nonlinearities in the relation, in the monthly regressions we first express each explanatory variable in terms of its ordinal ranking and then scale it to lie between zero and one. This has the added benefit of expressing all the explanatory variables on a common scale, so that their coefficients can be directly compared. The dependent variable is either the buy-and-hold return over the subsequent six months or over the first postformation year. Table 8.7 reports the time-series averages of the slope coefficients, and their *t*-statistics. Since the dependent variable in each monthly regression is a return measured over overlapping intervals, the *t*-statistics are corrected for autocorrelation. The standard error of the time series of coefficients from the regression for six-month (twelve-month) returns is adjusted for a fifth-order (eleventh-order) moving average process.

Prior return and earnings surprise, taken separately, are each strongly and positively related to future six-month returns (Panel A). The average slope from the regressions of returns on prior return alone is 5.7 percent, which is 4.1 times its standard error. In comparison, using either SUE or REV6 as the predictor variable gives very similar average slopes (6 percent), while the average slope for ABR is smaller (3.7 percent). In all cases, the coefficients are large relative to their standard errors.

The regression with all three measures of earnings surprise yields average slopes that are reliably different from zero, confirming our earlier impression that each adds information not contained in the other two. All four momentum variables are considered simultaneously in the last regression. Earnings surprises rob past return of some, but not all, of its predictive power. The coefficient for prior return falls from 5.7 percent when it is the only momentum variable to 2.9 percent in the full regression model. In this latter equation, past standardized unexpected earnings and revisions in analysts' forecasts, with average coefficients of 3.2 and 3.1 percent, respectively, are just as important as prior return in predicting returns over the following six months.

The results from regressions for twelve-month returns are reported in Panel B of Table 8.7. When past return is the only momentum variable, its average slope is 10.3 percent. Introducing earnings surprises into the equation knocks the estimated effect down to 7.6 percent. Nonetheless, the average slope on past return is large not only relative to its standard error, but also compared to the slopes on the other earnings surprise variables in the last regression. The continu-

Table 8.7

Monthly Cross-Sectional Regressions of Returns on Prior Return and Prior Earnings Surprises

Cross-sectional regressions are estimated each month from January 1977 to January 1993 of individual stock returns on size, compound return over the prior six months (R^6), the abnormal return relative to the equally weighted market index cumulated from two days before to one day after the most recent past announcement date of quarterly earnings (ABR), unexpected earnings (the change in the most recent past quarterly earnings per share from its value four quarters ago) scaled by the standard deviation of unexpected earnings over the past eight quarters (SUE), and a moving average of the past six months' revisions in I/B/E/S mean analysts' earnings forecasts relative to beginning-of-month stock price (REV6). In the regression each explanatory variable is expressed in terms of its percentile rank and scaled to fall between zero and one. The dependent variable is the stock's buy-and-hold return either over the subsequent six months (Panel A), or over the next year (Panel B). The reported statistics are the means of the time series of coefficients from the month-by-month regressions, and in parentheses the t-statistics relative to the autocorrelation-adjusted standard error of the mean. The sample includes all domestic primary firms on New York Stock Exchange (NYSE), American Stock Exchange (AMEX), and Nasdaq with coverage on the Center for Research in Security Prices (CRSP) and COMPUSTAT.

Intercept	Size	R6	ABR	SUE	REV6
Panel A: Dependent Variable: Six-Month Return					
0.085	−0.037	0.057			
(2.50)	(−1.42)	(4.07)			
0.093	−0.033		0.037		
(2.82)	(−1.22)		(9.25)		
0.085	−0.041			0.060	
(2.50)	(−1.52)			(6.00)	
0.086	−0.042				0.060
(2.46)	(−1.62)				(5.45)
0.067	−0.044		0.022	0.037	0.040
(1.97)	(−1.69)		(4.40)	(4.63)	(4.00)
0.062	−0.044	0.029	0.017	0.032	0.031
(1.82)	(−1.69)	(2.07)	(4.25)	(4.00)	(3.10)
Panel B: Dependent Variable: One-Year Return					
0.190	−0.084	0.103			
(2.88)	(−1.33)	(3.96)			
0.209	−0.075		0.055		
(3.22)	(−1.14)		(7.86)		
0.206	−0.084			0.071	
(3.12)	(−1.27)			(4.18)	
0.205	−0.085				0.076
(3.01)	(−1.33)				(3.80)

131

Table 8.7 *(continued)*

Intercept	Size	R6	ABR	SUE	REV6
0.179	−0.087		0.038	0.037	0.054
(2.63)	(−1.36)		(5.43)	(2.64)	(3.00)
0.166	−0.089	0.076	0.026	0.026	0.031
(2.44)	(−1.41)	(3.17)	(3.71)	(2.00)	(1.94)

ation in stock price movements over the intermediate term includes a component unrelated to the news in near-term earnings. Finally, a comparison of the results in the two panels reinforces the impression from the earlier sections that price momentum tends to have longer-lasting effects than earnings momentum.

IV. Are Price and Earnings Momentum Subsequently Corrected?

One way to distinguish between some of the competing explanations for continuations in price movements is to examine whether there is a subsequent correction in the stock price.

In the one-way classifications by prior return (Table 8.2), it is hard to find direct evidence of return reversals in the years following portfolio formation. The raw returns in the second and third following years are not very different across portfolios. There is, however, some tendency for the extreme decile portfolios to concentrate on smaller stocks. The stocks in portfolios 1 and 10 have an average size decile ranking of 2.9, while the average size decile ranking of the stocks in the other portfolios lies between 3.7 and 4.4. The size rankings are based on the breakpoints from the distribution of market capitalization for NYSE stocks. The smaller average capitalization of stocks in the winner portfolio pulls their average return in one direction, but at the same time their lower book-to-market ratio pulls the return in the other direction. All in all, the picture with respect to reversals in the return on the winner portfolio is muddy. On the other hand, the raw returns on the loser portfolio in the following years tend to stay low (the more so taking into account the smaller average capitalization and higher book-to-market ratio of portfolio 1). The lack of direct evidence on reversals tends to call into question the hypothesis that the continuation in prices is induced by positive feedback trading.

Similarly, the one-way sorts by prior earnings surprise (Tables 8.3 to 8.5) also fail to turn up signs of subsequent return reversals. Future returns to stocks with bad news about earnings tend to stay relatively low. For both price and earnings momentum, therefore, there do not seem to be any price corrections in subsequent years.

The two-way classifications in Table 8.6 give a sharper verdict on whether the movement in prices is permanent or transitory. Although the portfolios that are ranked highest by both prior return and earnings surprise always have the largest return in the first following year, their returns are not much different from average in the second and third following years. For example portfolio (3, 3) in Panel B of the table has a return of 19.9 percent in the second year, compared to the overall mean return that year of 19.6 percent for all stocks in the sample; its return in the third year is 20 percent compared to 19.5 percent for the entire sample.

At the other end of the scale, the persistence in poor performance is striking. In particular, the doubly afflicted portfolio (1, 1), with poor past price performance and bad earnings news, continues to suffer a drawn-out decline. Even two and three years after portfolio formation, the portfolio's returns in Panels A to C continue to fall below the average. In Panel C, for instance, the returns for portfolio (1, 1) are 16.9 percent and 16.4 percent in the second and third years respectively, which are the lowest returns in each year across the nine portfolios in the panel. The shortfall in returns would be even more dramatic if the small size and high book-to-market ratio of the loser portfolio were to be taken into account. It might be argued that a more rapid adjustment in the prices of these poorly performing stocks runs up against several obstacles: it is more difficult to enter into short positions than long positions, and security analysts, as we have noted above, tend to acknowledge only gradually the negative prospects for these firms.

In the case of stocks that are ranked highest by prior return, an interesting dichotomy emerges when we condition on whether the past returns are confirmed by earnings news. For example, for those cases in Panel A where the stock is ranked highest by prior return and, in addition, the high past-returns are validated by high announcement returns (portfolio (3, 3)), the average first-year return is 27 percent. When the earnings news does not confirm the past returns (portfolio 1,3)), however, the average first-year return is 21.3 percent, which is only slightly higher than the overall mean first-year return of 20 percent across all stocks in the sample. By the second year, the return on portfolio (1, 3) is 18.3 percent, which is below the overall average of 19.6 percent, while the return on the twice-favored portfolio (3, 3) is about 20 percent. In the same fashion, the results in Panels B and C confirm a reversal in returns in the second year for those cases where high past returns are not supported by similarly favorable news about earnings. Much of the performance of stocks with high price momentum thus occurs when high prior returns are accompanied by favorable news about earnings.

V. OTHER TESTS

A. Price and Earnings Momentum for Large Stocks

In this section, we apply our momentum strategies to a sample composed of larger stocks only. Limiting attention to the larger stocks helps to alleviate potential problems of survivor bias in the sample, and problems with low-priced stocks.[10] Stocks with higher market capitalization are also of more interest to institutional investors.

In Tables 8.8 and 8.9, the sample comprises stocks whose market capitalization as of the portfolio formation date exceeds the median market value of NYSE stocks. In order to minimize repetition, we report results only for returns in the first year following portfolio formation. Even for this set of large firms, which are more widely

---

[10]In the last portfolio formation period, there are only two stocks in our large-stock sample (out of about a thousand eligible stocks) that have prices below five dollars.

Table 8.8

Mean Returns for Portfolios Based on Large Firms

The sample includes all New York Stock Exchange (NYSE), American Stock Exchange (AMEX), and Nasdaq domestic primary issues with coverage on the Center for Research in Security Prices (CRSP) and COMPUSTAT, and with beginning-of-month market value of equity above the median market capitalization of NYSE issues. Eligible stocks are ranked and grouped into portfolios on the basis of one classification variable (Panel A) or two classification variables (Panel B). Portfolios are formed at the beginning of every month from January 1977 to January 1993. The assignment of stocks to portfolios uses breakpoints based on NYSE issues only. All stocks are equally weighted in a portfolio, and average buy-and-hold returns are reported for the first year after portfolio formation. In Panel A the classification variable is either the stock's compound return over the prior six months (R6), standardized unexpected earnings (SUE, the change in most recently announced quarterly earnings per share from its value four quarters ago, divided by the standard deviation of unexpected earnings over the past eight quarters), abnormal returns relative to the equally weighted market index cumulated from two days before to one day after the date of the most recent past earnings announcement (ABR), or a moving average of the prior six months' percentage revisions relative to the beginning-of-month stock price in mean I/B/E/S estimates of current fiscal-year earnings per share (REV6). In Panel B, portfolios are formed from the intersections of independent sorts by prior return and by one measure of earnings surprise (standardized unexpected earnings, cumulative abnormal return around earnings announcement, or moving average of analysts' revisions).

Panel A: Mean Return in First Postformation Year from One-Way Classifications

Ranked by: (Low)	1	2	3	4	5	6	7	8	9	10 (High)
Prior 6-month return	0.086	0.145	0.156	0.170	0.176	0.176	0.182	0.188	0.202	0.226
Standardized unexpected earnings	0.147	0.147	0.168	0.171	0.183	0.187	0.183	0.190	0.192	0.176
Abnormal announcement return	0.140	0.163	0.171	0.173	0.177	0.183	0.175	0.187	0.180	0.183
Revision in analyst forecasts	0.134	0.154	0.163	0.162	0.163	0.174	0.177	0.181	0.191	0.210

Panel B: Mean Return in First Postformation Year from Two-Way Classifications

Earnings surprise rank	1 (Low)	2	3	1	2	3	1	2	3 (High)
Prior 6-month return rank	1 (Low)	1	1	2	2	2	3	3	3 (High)
Standardized unexpected earnings and prior return	0.133	0.154	0.136	0.162	0.180	0.186	0.175	0.209	0.210
Abnormal announcement return and prior return	0.135	0.143	0.125	0.168	0.181	0.179	0.190	0.197	0.219
Revision in analyst forecasts and prior return	0.128	0.139	0.131	0.164	0.175	0.190	0.200	0.191	0.213

Table 8.9

Monthly Cross-Sectional Regressions of Returns on Prior Return and Prior Earnings Surprises, Using Large Firms Only

The sample includes all New York Stock Exchange (NYSE), American Stock Exchange (AMEX), and Nasdaq domestic primary issues with coverage on the Center for Research in Security Prices (CRSP) and COMPUSTAT, and with beginning-of-month market value of equity above the median market capitalization of NYSE issues. Cross-sectional regressions are estimated each month from January 1977 to January 1993. The dependent variable is each stock's one-year buy-and-hold return. The explanatory variables are firm size and the following: R6 is the stock's compound return over the prior six months, SUE is the change in most recently announced quarterly earnings per share from its value four quarters ago, divided by the standard deviation of unexpected earnings over the past eight quarters, ABR is the abnormal return relative to the equally weighted market index cumulated from two days before to one day after the date of the most recent past earnings announcement, and REV6 is a moving average of the prior six months' percentage revisions relative to the beginning-of-month stock price in mean I/B/E/S estimates of current fiscal-year earnings per share. The reported statistics are the means of the time series of coefficients from the month-by-month regressions, and in parentheses the t-statistics relative to the autocorrelation-adjusted standard error of the mean.

Intercept	Size	R6	ABR	SUE	REV6
0.207	−0.093	0.084			
(3.23)	(−1.50)	(2.90)			
0.232	−0.093		0.036		
(3.52)	(−1.45)		(3.60)		
0.230	−0.097			0.044	
(3.33)	(−1.49)			(2.20)	
0.222	−0.096				0.058
(3.08)	(−1.50)				(2.07)
0.207	−0.097		0.026	0.020	0.043
(2.88)	(−1.54)		(2.89)	(1.33)	(1.65)
0.191	−0.094	0.064	0.015	0.015	0.023
(2.77)	(−1.54)	(2.21)	(1.67)	(1.07)	(0.92)

followed and for which timely information should be more readily available, there is still evidence that the market adjusts only gradually to the information in past returns or past earnings news. Notably, the one-way sorts in Panel A of Table 8.8 continue to deliver sizable differences in returns. This is particularly true when stocks are ranked by prior return; the spread in future one-year returns is 14 percent, which is almost as large as the spread for the entire sample in Table 8.2 (15.4 percent). A large difference in returns is also obtained when sorting on past analysts' revisions. The one-year spread in this case is 7.6 percent (compared to 9.7 percent for the entire sample in Table

8.5). When past SUE or past announcement return is the ranking variable, the one-year spreads are 2.9 and 4.3 percent, respectively (the corresponding spreads based on the entire sample are 7.5 and 8.3 percent).

Panel B of Table 8.8 replicates our two-way sorts on the larger stocks. Compared to the entire sample, the large-stock sample displays smaller differences in returns between the highest-ranked and lowest-ranked portfolios. Nonetheless, the spreads remain large: 8.4 percent for the two-way classification based on prior return and announcement return, 7.7 percent based on prior return and SUE, and 8.5 percent based on prior return and revisions in consensus estimates. Although sorting by prior return conditional on past earnings news gives rise to larger differences in subsequent returns, earnings surprises still have some marginal explanatory power. For example, the average one-year spread across prior return ranks, holding fixed the rank by standardized unexpected earnings, is 5.7 percent. The average spread associated with standardized unexpected earnings, conditional on prior return, is 2.1 percent. Earnings news has a lesser impact on the returns of large companies because there are numerous additional sources of information about the outlook for these companies.

Table 8.9 fits cross-sectional regressions to future twelve-month returns for the large-stock sample. The regressions support the results from the earlier panels in the table. In the univariate regressions, for example, each momentum variable is statistically significant. When they are considered together in the last regression, the most important variable is the prior six-month return; its average coefficient is 6.4 percent, which is more than two standard errors away from zero.

B. Adjusting for Size and Book-to-Market Factors

Our earlier results in Tables 8.2 to 8.5 raise the possibility that the predictive power of prior returns or prior earnings surprises may be confounded with the effects of book-to-market or firm size. In this section we investigate whether the behavior of returns on our different momentum portfolios can be explained by factors related to size and book-to-market. This is done in the context of the Fama-French (1993) three-factor model, given by time series regressions of the form

$$r_{pt} - r_{ft} = \alpha_p + \beta_p(r_{mt} - r_{ft}) + s_p\text{SMB}_t + h_p\text{HML}_t + \varepsilon_{pt} \qquad (4)$$

Here r_{pt} is the return on portfolio p in month t; r_{ft} and r_{mt} are the Treasury bill rate and the return on the value-weighted market index, respectively; SMB_t is the return on the mimicking portfolio for size; and HML_t is the return on the mimicking portfolio for book-to-market.[11] If the momentum strategies' performance is just a manifestation of size and book-to-market effects, then the intercept of the equation, α_p, should not be significantly different from zero.

Fama and French (1996) use equation (4) to analyze the performance of portfolios sorted by prior return. Here we examine the evidence when earnings momentum is brought into the picture as well.[12] In particular, we focus on the double-sort portfolios based on prior return and revisions in consensus estimates. Table 8.10 reports summary statistics of the time series regressions for the highest- and lowest-ranked portfolios (portfolios (3, 3) and (1, 1) respectively, in Panel C of Table 8.6). We track the monthly returns from a strategy of buying each portfolio and holding it for six months, when a new portfolio is formed and the process repeated. Table 8.10 also reports results for the arbitrage portfolio formed by buying the highest-ranked portfolio, or the winners, and selling the lowest-ranked portfolio, or the losers.

The portfolios of winners and losers have very similar market risk exposures (b_p). In other respects, the results in Table 8.10 generally confirm our earlier findings. Both portfolios load significantly on size.

---

[11]We thank Eugene Fama for providing the data on the mimicking portfolio returns.

[12]Fama and French (1994) report that the portfolio of losers, compared to the portfolio of winners, loads more heavily on the size and book-to-market factors. The difference in intercepts between the top and bottom deciles is 1.74 percent per month. We find quite similar results.

Table 8.10

Three-Factor Time Series Regressions Based on Monthly Excess Returns (in Percent) on Portfolios from Two-Way Classification by Prior Return and Analyst Revisions

The regression is estimated over monthly observations from January 1977 to December 1993. The dependent variable is the monthly return in excess of the Treasury-bill rate from a strategy of buying a portfolio of stocks ranked highest or lowest (winners and losers, respectively) from an independent sort on two classification variables. The classification variables are: the stock's compound return over the past six months, and a moving average of the past six months' percentage revisions relative to the beginning-of-month stock price in the mean I/B/E/S estimate of current fiscal-year earnings per share. The portfolio is held for six months, at which time the portfolio is reformed and the strategy repeated. The explanatory variables are the monthly returns from the Fama and French (1993) mimicking portfolios for size and book-to-market factors, and the monthly return in excess of the Treasury-bill rate on the value-weighted market portfolio of all the component stocks from the mimicking portfolios. Results are also presented for the difference between the two portfolios, i.e., the zero-cost portfolio of buying past winners and selling past losers. The regression R^2 is adjusted for degrees of freedom, and t-statistics are shown in parentheses below the coefficient estimates.

Portfolio	Intercept	Market	Size	Book-to-Market	R^2
Winners	0.478	1.041	0.782	−0.180	0.95
	(4.11)	(36.50)	(16.78)	(−3.47)	
Losers	−0.953	1.062	0.783	0.254	0.90
	(−6.08)	(27.55)	(12.43)	(3.61)	
Difference	1.431	−0.021	−0.001	−0.434	0.12
	(5.91)	(−0.35)	(−0.01)	(−4.00)	

The portfolio of winners concentrates more heavily on glamour stocks, so it loads negatively on the book-to-market factor, while the portfolio of losers is more oriented toward value stocks, and so loads positively on the book-to-market factor. The main conclusion from Table 8.10 is that adjusting for size and book-to-market does not change the observed pattern in returns. The intercept for the loser portfolio (−0.953 percent per month) is especially eye-catching. This poor performance stems from the fact that the loser portfolio has persistently low returns, even though it is tilted toward small stocks with high book-to-market ratios (which would tend to raise average returns). The intercept for the arbitrage portfolio is 1.43 percent, with a t-statistic of 5.91.

Past winners, if they are riskier than past losers, should have worse (better) performance in bad (good) states of the world, irrespective of the identity of the underlying risk factors. To the extent that bad and good states correspond to low and high excess returns, respectively, on a broad stock market index, we can check if this is the case. In particular, during months where the return on the CRSP value-weighted market index falls below the monthly Treasury-bill rate, riskier stocks should earn lower returns. As it turns out, during such down-market months the difference between the returns of the winner and loser portfolios from our two-way sort on prior return and analysts' revisions is positive (0.60 percent per month). Conversely, in up-market months (where the return on the value-weighted index exceeds the Treasury-bill rate) the average difference between the returns of the winner and loser portfolios is 1.79 percent. Strategies exploiting high momentum in stock prices thus seem to do especially well in up-markets. In any event, there is no evidence that the winner portfolio is exposed to larger downside risk.

VI. CONCLUSIONS

Unless we understand why a particular investment strategy works, we should be skeptical about its out-of-sample performance. There are several competing hypotheses concerning the profitability of contrarian strategies for short- or long-horizon returns. However, there is a glaring lack of explanations for the continuation in stock prices over intermediate horizons (short of sweeping the issue under the rug by relabeling the phenomenon as part of the "normal" cross section of expected returns). This paper fills in some of the gaps in our understanding of two major unresolved puzzles in the empirical finance literature: why two pieces of publicly available information—a stock's prior six-month return and the most recent earnings surprise—help to predict future returns. The drift in future returns is economically meaningful and lasts for at least six months. For example, sorting stocks by prior six-month return yields spreads in returns of 8.8 percent over the subsequent six months. Similarly, ranking stocks by a moving average of past revisions in consensus estimates of earnings produces spreads of 7.7 percent over the next six months. Our results are robust with respect to how we measure earnings surprise: as standardized unexpected earnings, abnormal returns around announcements of earnings, or revisions in analysts' forecasts of earnings. In general, the price momentum effect tends to be stronger and longer-lived than the earnings momentum effect.

The bulk of the evidence suggests that the drifts in future returns are not subsequently reversed, so momentum does not appear to be entirely driven by positive feedback trading. The price continuations are particularly notable for stocks with the worst past earnings performance, whose returns are below average for up to three years afterward. There is stronger evidence of subsequent correction in prices when large, positive prior returns are not validated by good news about earnings. In the first year following portfolio formation, stocks ranked highest by prior return but lowest by abnormal announcement return earn a rate of return (21.3 percent) that is not very different from the average of 20 percent. The fact that returns for the past winners are high only in the first subsequent year, but are not much different from the average in the second or third years, poses a challenge for risk-based explanations of the profitability of momentum strategies. More direct evidence from a three-factor model also suggests that the profitability cannot be explained by size and book-to-market effects.

An alternative explanation is that the market responds gradually to new information. Since earnings provide an ongoing source of information about a firm's prospects, we focus on the market's reaction when earnings are released. Indeed, a substantial portion of the momentum effect is concentrated around subsequent earnings announcements. For example, about 41 percent of the superior performance in the first six months of the price momentum strategy occurs around the announcement dates of earnings. More generally, if the market is surprised by good or bad earnings news, then on average the market continues to be surprised in the same direction at least over the next two subsequent announcements. Clearly, however, the return on a stock also incorporates numerous other sources of news that are not directly related to near-term earnings: stock buybacks, insider trading, and new equity issues, for example. The large drifts in future returns thus paint a picture of a market which underreacts.

Another piece of evidence compatible with the sluggish response of market participants is the prolonged adjustment of analysts' forecasts. The inertia in revising forecasts may not be helping the market to assimilate new information in a timely fashion. In particular, analysts are especially slow in revising their estimates in the case of companies with the worst performance. This may possibly be due to their reluctance to alienate management.

When we disentangle the sources of the momentum strategies' performance, we find that each of the variables we analyze—prior return, as well as each of the earnings surprise variables considered—has marginal predictive power for the postformation drifts in returns. In cross-sectional regressions of future six-month returns on past returns, the coefficient on prior return is 5.7 percent. Introducing past earnings surprises lowers the coefficient to 2.9 percent, although it is still reliably nonzero. Each momentum strategy thus draws upon the market's underreaction to different pieces of information.

Our evidence that the market's response to news takes time is not an entirely negative verdict on the informational efficiency of the stock market. Note that prior news has already caused a substantial realignment in stock prices over the preceding six months. In Table 8.2, for instance, the past adjustment produces differences in returns of roughly 100 percent between the most favorably and least favorably affected stocks. Put in this perspective, the remaining adjustment that is left on the table for investors, as measured by the spread in future one-year returns of about 15 percent, becomes less striking.

A note of caution is necessary. The spreads we document here for momentum strategies may not be fully capturable. Given the constraints many investors face, it may not be feasible to establish short positions in stocks with low momentum. A momentum strategy is trading-intensive, and stocks with high momentum tend to be smaller issues whose trading costs tend to be relatively high. These implementation issues will reduce the benefits from pursuing momentum strategies. To illustrate the point, suppose an investor wishes to exploit price momentum by buying the top two deciles of stocks ranked by prior return in Table 8.2 (so as to have a relatively well-diversified portfolio). This would yield an average annual return of about

27 percent. If the relevant benchmark is the average return across all the eligible stocks in Table 8.2, roughly 22 percent, this investor earns an extra 5 percent. Chan and Lakonishok (1995) report average trading costs for small firms of about 3 percent (combining a purchase and a sale), so the extra returns for a momentum strategy are substantially reduced after accounting for trading costs.

Finally, our evidence of underreaction over intermediate horizons suggests that a stock with low past returns will on average experience low subsequent returns. It might be argued that a contrarian overreaction story would instead predict high subsequent returns for such a stock. Is there any contradiction between the two stories? A full reconciliation of these two bodies of evidence is beyond the scope of this article, but we suggest that they may not be incompatible. The common element is the market's tendency to anchor too heavily on past trends. Investors discount new information that is at odds with their mindsets and change their perceptions gradually.

Stocks selected under a momentum strategy, however, carry along a very different set of investor perceptions from stocks selected under a contrarian strategy. Our price momentum strategy identifies low-momentum stocks, for example, on the basis of poor returns over the immediate past (the prior six months). On looking at their experience over a more extended past period, however, these stocks are on average not much different from other stocks, so investors extrapolate from the past and perceive them as "normal" stocks. For example, the compound rate of return beginning three years and ending six months before portfolio formation is about 61 percent for the portfolio with the lowest past six-month price momentum, compared to the average of 62 percent over all stocks. Given this mindset, when disappointing news arrives, investors initially discount the information. This gives rise to a subsequent downward drift in prices.

In contrast, a contrarian strategy focuses on stocks that have extremely poor returns over a prolonged past period. The history of disappointments creates an investor mindset of excessive pessimism. This may be reinforced by money managers' unwillingness to be regarded as holding an "imprudent" investment that might fall into distress. These companies, however, are not as poor investment prospects as the market perceives them to be. Rather, it takes time for these stocks to shake off the unfavorable opinions that investors have accumulated. LaPorta, Lakonishok, Shleifer, and Vishny (1995) study such stocks and find that the market's learning about future earnings prospects is a long and very drawn-out process, lasting for a few years. This sets the stage for subsequent reversals in prices that may persist for several years. As in the case of low-momentum stocks, the reversals are a result of investors' tendency of over-weight the past and extrapolate too far into the future. This line of thinking is, admittedly, only suggestive. Spelling out the links between momentum strategies and contrarian strategies remains an important open area of research.

REFERENCES

Affleck-Graves, John, and Richard R. Mendenhall, 1992, The relation between the Value Line enigma and post-earnings-announcement drift, *Journal of Financial Economics* 31, 75–96.

Ball, Ray, and S. P. Kothari, 1989, Nonstationary expected returns: Implications for tests of market efficiency and serial correlations in returns, *Journal of Financial Economics* 25, 51–74.

Ball, Ray, S. P. Kothari, and Jay Shanken, 1995, Problems in measuring portfolio performance: An application to contrarian investment strategies, *Journal of Financial Economics* 38, 79–107.

Bernard, Victor L., and Jacob K. Thomas, 1989, Post-earnings-announcement drift: Delayed price response or risk premium? *Journal of Accounting Research (Supplement)* 27, 1–36.

Bernard, Victor L., Jacob K. Thomas, and James Wahlen, 1995, Accounting-based stock price anomalies: Separating market inefficiencies from research design flaws. Working paper, University of Michigan.

Chan, Louis K. C., Yasushi Hamao, and Josef Lakonishok, 1991, Fundamentals and stock returns in Japan, *Journal of Finance* 46, 1739–1764.

Chan, Louis K. C., and Josef Lakonishok, 1995, A cross-market comparison of institutional equity trading costs. Working paper, University of Illinois.

Chari, V. V., Ravi Jagannathan, and Aharon R. Ofer, 1988, Seasonalities in security returns: The case of earnings announcements, *Journal of Financial Economics* 21, 101–121.

Chopra, Navin, Josef Lakonishok, and Jay R. Ritter, 1992, Measuring abnormal performance: Do stocks overreact? *Journal of Financial Economics* 31, 235–268.

Conrad, Jennifer, and Gautam Kaul, 1993, Long-term market overreaction or biases in computed returns? *Journal of Finance* 48, 39–64.

DeBondt, Werner F. M., and Richard H. Thaler, 1985, Does the stock market overreact? *Journal of Finance* 40, 793–805.

DeBondt, Werner F. M., and Richard H. Thaler, 1987, Further evidence on investor overreaction and stock market seasonality, *Journal of Finance* 42, 557–581.

DeLong, J. Bradford, Andrei Shleifer, Lawrence H. Summers, and Robert J. Waldmann, 1990, Positive feedback investment strategies and destabilizing rational speculation, *Journal of Finance* 45, 379–395.

Fama, Eugene F., 1991, Efficient capital markets: II, *Journal of Finance* 46, 1575–1617.

Fama, Eugene F., and Kenneth R. French, 1992, The cross-section of expected stock returns, *Journal of Finance* 47, 427–465.

Fama, Eugene F., and Kenneth R. French, 1993, Common risk factors in the returns on stocks and bonds, *Journal of Financial Economics* 33, 3–56.

Fama, Eugene F., and Kenneth R. French, 1995, Size and book-to-market factors in earnings and returns, *Journal of Finance* 50, 131–155.

Fama, Eugene F., and Kenneth R. French, 1996, Multifactor explanations of asset pricing anomalies, *Journal of Finance* 51, 55–84.

Fama, Eugene F., and James MacBeth, 1973, Risk, return and equilibrium: Empirical tests, *Journal of Political Economy* 81, 607–636.

Foster, George, Chris Olsen, and Terry Shevlin, 1984, Earnings releases, anomalies, and the behavior of security returns, *The Accounting Review* 59, 574–603.

Givoly, Dan, and Josef Lakonishok, 1979, The information content of financial analysts' forecasts of earnings: Some evidence on semi-strong inefficiency, *Journal of Accounting and Economics* 1, 165–185.

Jegadeesh, Narasimhan, 1990, Evidence of predictable behavior of security returns, *Journal of Finance* 45, 881–898.

Jegadeesh, Narasimhan, and Sheridan Titman, 1993, Returns to buying winners and selling losers: Implications for stock market efficiency, *Journal of Finance* 48, 65–91.

Jegadeesh, Narasimhan, and Sheridan Titman, 1995, Short-horizon return reversals and the bid-ask spread, *Journal of Financial Intermediation* 4, 116–132.

Jones, Charles P., and Robert H. Litzenberger, 1970, Quarterly earnings reports and intermediate stock price trends, *Journal of Finance* 25, 143–148.

Kaul, Gautam, and M. Nimalendran, 1990, Price reversals: Bid-ask errors or market overreaction? *Journal of Financial Economics* 28, 67–93.

Klein, April, 1990, A direct test of the cognitive bias theory of share price reversals, *Journal of Accounting and Economics* 13, 155–166.

Lakonishok, Josef, Andrei Shleifer, and Robert W. Vishny, 1994, Contrarian investment, extrapolation, and risk, *Journal of Finance* 49, 1541–1578.

Lakonishok, Josef, and Seymour Smidt, 1986, Capital gain taxation and volume of trading, *Journal of Finance* 41, 951–976.

LaPorta, Rafael, Josef Lakonishok, Andrei Shleifer, and Robert W. Vishny, 1995. Good news for value stocks: Further evidence on market efficiency. Working paper, University of Illinois.

Latane, Henry A., and Charles P. Jones, 1979, Standardized unexpected earnings–1971–1977, *Journal of Finance* 34, 717–724.

Lehmann, Bruce N., 1990, Fads, martingales and market efficiency, *Quarterly Journal of Economics* 60, 1–28.

Lo, Andrew W., and A. Craig MacKinlay, 1990, When are contrarian profits due to stock market overrreaction? *Review of Financial Studies* 3, 175–205.

Womack, Kent L., 1996, Do brokerage analysts' recommendations have investment value? *Journal of Finance* forthcoming.

CHAPTER 9

The Misuse of
Past-Performance Data

Mark Hulbert

INTRODUCTION

Let me start by describing what I do so you can better understand the basis for what I plan to say about the misuse of past-performance data. Let me stress that I am not an advisor myself. I don't claim any market-timing ability or knack for picking individual stocks. In fact, I should let you know that I have been personally bearish for most of the past 16 years. So if I'd been an advisor, my clients would have lost out on one of the most dynamic bull markets. However, what I have done over these 16 years is objectively track the performance of those who *do* think they know which way the market is going and which stocks and strategies will end up beating the market. I've been reporting the results in the *Hulbert Financial Digest* (HFD).

To calculate the performance ratings of various newsletters, my company goes to great lengths. For example, we use the stock prices that prevail on the day a reader could actually act on a newsletter's advice because our goal is to reflect the real-world worth of a strategy to a typical reader. But achieving this goal has turned out to be quite complicated: We began to notice that newsletters that were otherwise quite honest and forthright about reporting their track records, warts and all, were nevertheless using the prices that prevailed on the day they said they first thought about their recommendations in their offices. These prices invariably were better than those a reader could have obtained by acting the day he or she received the newsletter in the mail.

You might think that overcoming this difficulty would require us only to note the dates on which we received the newsletters at the HFD office. But it isn't that easy. Imagine what would happen if a newsletter editor recommended a thinly traded stock in a particular issue that was sent to us several days in advance of being sent to regular subscribers. The HFD dutifully would buy this position at the price prevailing on the date of receipt, and the stock would undoubtedly shoot up in price several days later when the newsletter's other subscribers bought it. In that event, the HFD's performance ratings would not be particularly relevant to the individual investor. To immunize us from that vulnerability, the HFD has had to subscribe to newsletters using anonymous names at different zip codes around the country. We currently spend over $20,000 per year fulfilling just this one part of our mission.

Another illustration of the care with which we construct performance ratings is that we call the telephone hotlines of the newsletters that offer them. Currently, about half of the 165 newsletters we track offer them, and they are updated as often as daily. We have a staff that comes in as early as 7:00 A.M. Eastern time every business day to call these hotlines, tape record them, and transcribe their recommendations so that we know exactly what subscribers to each newsletter have been advised to do.

In sum, what we have done is construct one of the world's largest databases of buy-and-sell signals from a very dynamic sector of the advisory industry. Although newsletters do not constitute a majority of the investment advisory industry by any means, they are in many ways representative of the industry as a whole as you'll see in a minute. Furthermore, our database is updated daily, whereas most of the academic databases on the performance of money managers are updated only quarterly (at the times the Securities and Exchange Commission (SEC) requires that they report the composition of their portfolios). I can't overestimate the value of the HFD's database being updated in real time. Most of the academic studies up to now have had to assume that the portfolios they're studying remain static for a quarter and then, at the end of the quarter, make one wholesale shift into some new portfolio configuration. In contrast, the HFD's database reflects portfolio changes however often the newsletter editors make new recommendations, which in some cases is three or four times a day.

THE MISUSE OF PAST-PERFORMANCE DATA

Let me start this discussion by focusing on examples from outside the finance arena and then applying those examples to the field of investing. Consider this: Psychologists discovered years ago that human beings find it impossible to contemplate true randomness. When seeing a set of random events, they nevertheless think that there is a pattern implicit in it. In one famous study, for example, subjects were asked to construct a random sequence and found it impossible. After a while the subjects would start introducing patterns, implicitly and unconsciously, into the series that was supposed to be random.

Another example is called the "gambler's fallacy." After flipping a coin four times and getting four heads in a row, a subject is asked the chances of getting tails on the fifth flip. The overwhelming answer given is that the fifth flip will be tails. The real answer is that each one of the five flips is absolutely independent, and the chance of tails is 50/50 on each flip.

Another great example is from sports. A number of years ago, a researcher studied the Philadelphia 76ers at a time when Julius Erving was their star player. He first asked a number of the spectators about Julius Erving's shooting patterns: If he made (scored on) four shots in a row, for example, what were his chances of making the fifth shot? Similarly, what were his chances if he had just missed four shots in a row? The fans definitely thought there would be a difference: If Erving made four or five shots in a row, his chances of making the next shot were much higher than his season-long average, and if he missed four or five in a row, his chances of making the next one were much lower than average. The researcher also asked the same questions to the players themselves. They answered that they absolutely would be more inclined to pass the ball to Erving if he had just made five shots in a row and less likely if he had just missed five in a row. Why? Because Erving would be playing either a hot or a a cold hand.

The researcher's next step was to analyze Erving's shooting statistics, and he discovered that no such phenomenon as a hot or cold hand existed. If Erving's season-long average was to complete 60 percent of his shots, for example, then his chances of hitting the sixth shot after hitting five shots in a row was statistically no different than 60 percent. Likewise, if he had just missed five shots in a row, his chances of hitting the sixth shot were statistically no different than 60 percent.

This definitely should give us pause. Here was something that people absolutely were sure existed, and yet it didn't. Once again we need to realize that we have no problem discovering patterns even when none exists.

It's always fun to look at these examples from outside of investing and laugh knowingly—as though we don't do the same thing when investing. But that would be missing the point: These examples suggest to us that we ourselves are most likely guilty of the same thing in the financial arena. Indeed, one of the most common mistakes people make when judging an advisor's record is to believe in the existence of hot or cold hands. Investors too often conclude that if an advisor beats the market over a quarter or over a six-month period, that advisor ought to be followed—just as Julius Erving's team members concluded after Erving hit a number of basketball shots in a row.

To those who have a hard time giving up the notion that advisors play hot and cold hands, I offer a rigorous statistical test known as the *Runs Test*. By applying this test to a set of data, it's possible to measure objectively whether there is a nonrandom run (or series)—regardless of whether that run is a series of coin flips or an investment advisor's performance. I've applied the Runs Test to my 16-year database of newsletter performance, and there is no evidence that any newsletter plays a hot or a cold hand. For example, over the past 10 years we have performance data for 89 newsletters. Of those, three pass the test. But there's less here than meets the eye. At the 95 percent confidence level, you would expect 4 of those 89 to come out as false-positives. So for the trailing 10-year period, there's no evidence of runs of luck or runs of skill, either on the winning side or on the losing side. The data over the past five years present the same picture: of the 219 portfolios for which the HFD has data, 10 look like they had significant runs. But at the 95 percent confidence level you would still expect 11 of the 219 to come out as false-positives. So there's really no evidence that there are runs of luck or of skill among investment advisors.

Nevertheless, over and over again I read that because some newsletter is doing fantastically, its editor must be playing a hot hand. A recent example is Carlton Lutts, who is the editor of the *Cabot Market Letter*. In 1995 his newsletter was the number-two performing newsletter among all that we track, with a gain of 53.6 percent—in contrast to a gain of 36.5 percent for the Wilshire 5000 index. As a result, his name was in neon, and my impression is that a number of investors decided to subscribe to the *Cabot Marketletter*. Yet these investors didn't bother to look at the fact that he was one of the worst performers in 1994, the year immediately prior. Nor did they focus on the fact that his 15-year return was well below a buy-and-hold. Everyone focused on what he was doing in 1995 alone. To be sure, for a while in 1996 it looked as though Lutts was continuing to play a hot hand when a couple of his stock picks enjoyed spectacular runs. But it didn't surprise me at all that those two stocks fizzled out and that Lutts's 1996 performance took a quick nosedive.

HOW LONG IS LONG TERM?

There are other misuses of performance data. One is based on the belief that short-term performance has significance. To illustrate the pitfalls of such a belief, consider the following. Imagine that one year into my tracking, which would have been on June 30, 1981, you constructed a portfolio that was divided equally among all newsletters that had beaten the market over the first year we tracked newsletters. And imagine further that you followed those winning newsletters for a year until June 30, 1982, and then switched your portfolio again into those newsletters that had beaten the market over the previous 12 months. By following such a strategy until today, you would have nearly 15 years of performance of this strategy of following the 12-month market beaters. Over these nearly 15 years, this portfolio would have gained about 95 percent. Note carefully: that's not 95 percent annualized, but a total of ninety-five percent during the most dynamic bull market we'll ever see in our lifetimes. That return compounds out to about 4 or 5 percent a year. You would have done better simply by investing in a money market fund.

Consider next what would have happened if, in contrast to investing with the 12-month market beaters, you instead had invested with the 12 month market laggards. That is, every June 30th you switched your portfolio into following those newsletters that had failed to beat the market on a trailing 12 month basis. That portfolio would now be up some 330 percent, a lot better than the 95 percent return realized by following the 12-month market beaters. Let me hasten to add, however, that you should not conclude from this that you should be following the 12-month market laggards. Bear in mind that the market itself is up about 550 percent over this 15-year period.

The overwhelming conclusion to draw is that 12-month gains are very unhelpful as a basis for picking an advisor for the future. You ought to be judging advisors on the basis of performance over a much longer period of time. But how long do you need to look before you start getting statistical significance? My work suggests it's a lot longer than any of us ever thought.

I have reached this conclusion by using a statistical measurement that allows us to determine the degree to which rankings are correlated. For example, if you look at one-year rankings and correlate them with future one-year rankings, you'd find a correlation coefficient that statistically is zero. That means there is no statistical relationship between a newsletter's rank in one year and its rank in the subsequent year. What about three years? What are the correlation coefficients when a ranking of newsletters for a previous three-year period is correlated with a ranking of those same newsletters over the next three-year period? I've measured it over every possible pairing of three year periods over the past 16 years, and on average the correlation coefficient is around 0.20, which in itself is barely statistically significant. But even assuming that it has statistical significance, its real-world significance is minimal: a coefficient of 0.20 corresponds to an r-squared of just 4 percent. That means that three-year rankings explain or predict just 4% of where an advisor will rank in the subsequent three-year period.

How about five years? If you look at all possible pairings of five year periods over the past 16 years, you come up with a correlation coefficient of about 0.25. That corresponds to an r-squared of 6 percent, which means that five-year rankings explain or predict just 6 percent of rankings over the subsequent five years.

To be sure, explaining 6 percent of the future is better than explaining nothing. But most people would have guessed that five years would have more explanatory power than this. A large proportion of investors who pick an advisor on the basis of past performance, for example, focus on five-year returns. A lot of people look at three years. And yet my data show that performance over that period of time has dramatically little statistical significance and even less real-world value. Yet people are out there betting on that basis all the time.

This analysis leads us straight into the horns of a dilemma. Once we realize that we must focus on performance over periods longer than five years, we dramatically reduce the scope of our analysis. For example, not only is ten years beyond the time horizon of the typical individual investor, it is longer than the tenure of the typical mutual fund or pension fund manager.

Consider a question that was posed several years ago to a group of statisticians: Over how long a period must an advisor beat the market to satisfy them at the 95 percent confidence level? When would the statisticians believe that the advisor had genuine ability? The statisticians looked at a number of different hypothetical cases.

Their first hypothetical case: beating the market by 1 percent annually. By the way, an advisor who can produce this return already is in the upper echelon of money managers because we know that 80 percent of money managers don't even beat the market. So if you beat the market by 1 percent a year, you're already at about the 90th percentile among money managers. According to the study, you would need 308 years of beating the market by 1 percent annually to satisfy a statistician at the 95 percent confidence level.

According to the statisticians, the only way in which you can get assurance in our lifetime at the 95 percent confidence level that an advisor has genuine ability is to beat the market by around 12 percent a year. In such a case, the statisticians would be satisfied after only a dozen years of beating the market. But this provides little solace. Warren Buffett might satisfy this precondition, but he's definitely the exception that proves the rule.

THE VIRTUES OF DISCIPLINE

You might be inclined to conclude at this point that you should just throw up your hands in despair. After all, you might now be asking, isn't everything we see random? But that's not the truth either. Just because people tend to see patterns in random events where there are no patterns doesn't mean that patterns don't exist.

In other words, not only must we guard against false-positives (detecting patterns where none exists), we also must guard against false-negatives (interpreting everything as random, including nonrandom events). And in guarding against false-negatives, statistics aren't as much help as you might think. After all, a statistician intent on interpreting an event as random always can find a story to tell about that event in which statistically it must be seen as random. But that doesn't always mean that that event is random.

The antidote to false-negatives in the investment arena is *discipline.* This is because the intellect itself sometimes is powerless to overcome false-negatives. After all, the overzealous statistician who forever detects randomness is nevertheless being intellectually rigorous.

To appreciate the benefits of discipline, let's assume you thought Treasury-bond (T-bond) rates would be at 4 percent sometime next year. Let's say you adopt a discipline for exploiting this assumption: Whenever rates deviate from 4 percent by a small enough amount, you buy T-bonds, and you sell them when rates deviate by large enough amounts. It's possible that such a discipline could produce a profit even if T-bonds didn't go to 4 percent next year. Why is this so? Because such a discipline forces you to buy low and sell high. It enables you to capitalize on what we know to be true psychologically—that the markets tend to oscillate back and forth between the extremes of under- and overreaction, between greed and fear. Markets overreact and then they underreact. Between those two extremes almost any discipline will probably capture something.

Let me hasten to stress that, in extolling the virtues of discipline, I'm not arguing that the intellect is worthless. Instead, my position is that the intellect alone isn't enough. Discipline is needed, too.

Another perspective on the virtues of discipline comes from the best performing newsletters over the past 15 years. On the whole, these newsletters are the ones that had a better adherence to discipline. In contrast, a number of their poorer-performing brethren pursue perfectly reasonable approaches with good long-term value, and instead of adhering to the discipline imposed by their approaches, their editors chose to second-guess their system. Almost invariably they ended up regretting that second-guessing. It's not hard to surmise why: They were tempted to second-guess when their psychological motivations were at their most self-destructive. They didn't second-guess when their strategies were winning. Instead, they second-guessed when they were losing, at which times their egos were invested in recovering their losses.

Consider discipline's role in the performance of the *Value Line Investment Survey*, which is the number-one performing newsletter since 1980. It has a great long-term record going back to 1965, one that's been verified by any number of different studies. Despite this great long-term record, however, *Value Line* has needed a strong discipline to adhere to its stock-picking methodology along the way.

This need for discipline arises because *Value Line* has not beaten the market every quarter or every calendar year along the way. This isn't a criticism but simply a statement of fact: there's no advisor who has ever existed or who ever will exist who beats the market in every short-term period. But these short-term market-lagging periods put enormous pressure on *Value Line* to start second-guessing its system. *Value Line* has more than 100,000 subscribers, it has several different mutual funds, and it's a publicly-traded company with shareholders who are upset when there's a lot of bad publicity.

Consider this: several years ago, *Value Line*'s ranking system was performing in just the opposite way from what it was supposed to do. Their Group 5 stocks (supposedly their worst bets) were doing better for the first half of the year than their Group 1 stocks (their best bests). A major newspaper ran an article speculating whether *Value Line* had lost its touch. That's bad publicity for anyone, but when you're a publicly traded company, even if you have a great long-term record, it's particularly tough. Even though six months of underperformance has absolutely no statistical significance, *Value Line* was under enormous pressure to second-guess its stock-ranking system.

But they didn't change—because of discipline. Their research director had a ready response to all who suggested changes: *Value Line* will alter its stock-picking methodology if it can be shown that the ranking system, as altered, would have done better than it actually did over the entire period since 1965.

Notice how strong a discipline this imposes. Though *Value Line* wasn't saying that it would never change, it was insisting that it wouldn't change just for short-term, ad-hoc reasons. In the end, *Value Line* didn't alter its ranking system. And it didn't surprise me that over the second half of that same year, *Value Line*'s performance recovered smartly, with its Group 1 stocks far outperforming their Group 5s.

Here is yet another perspective on the need for discipline: There are top performers who are fundamentalists, some who are technicians, and some who are chartists. By the same token, there are bottom performers who are fundamentalists, some who are technicians, and some who are chartists. Indeed, virtually every major investment approach is pursued by both a top-performing letter and a bottom-performing one. The inevitable conclusion is that in the right hands,

156

almost any method can work; and in the wrong hands, almost any method won't work. The difference has to do with something else. The something else is discipline.

I am much more inclined to follow a newsletter that has the courage and the discipline to stick with its system even during those short-term periods in which it isn't working. I am less inclined to follow an advisor who's changing his or her system according to whatever is the latest fashion on Wall Street. But adhering to a system when it isn't working takes an enormous commitment.

This same lesson also applies when the investor is picking a newsletter or a fund to follow. One consequence of the need for discipline is that you need to be willing to follow your chosen advisor for a lot longer than one year at a time. Picking an advisor may not exactly be the same as a marriage, but it's a lot closer to being a marriage than it is to being a one-night stand. Yet most people are picking advisors as though the relationship were a one-night stand—and in the morning asking "What have you done for me lately?" As we discussed earlier, performance over the short term is basically noise. You need discipline so that you will adhere to your chosen advisor for a number of years so that you will give that advisor a chance to show his stuff.

Here's a good rule of thumb to help you develop good discipline yourself as an investor: Write down on a sheet of paper the criterion (or criteria) you use in picking an advisor. Get rid of that advisor in the future only when the fresh reapplication of those original criteria doesn't lead you to pick that same advisor.

This is where individual discipline comes in. Like Ulysses, you need to tie yourself to the mast to avoid the sirens' song. Yet our financial culture is full of siren songs. There are newsletters, magazines, television shows, and conferences talking about an endless number of new approaches to the market, and they all sound plausible. They all sound convincing, and they all contradict each other. So either you give up, or you find an anchor or ballast to avoid temptation. The only sure way to do that is by adopting discipline.

157

CHAPTER 10

Tilting the Investment Odds in Your Favor

Steven Halpern

We are at a fascinating point in stock market history. We are experiencing now more change in the way that markets operate than at any other time. The amount of information that is processed and the speed at which that information is disseminated in increasing at a mindboggling rate. Individuals with home computers can now access information that was previously available only to institutional traders. High-powered technical analysis is now available with a click of a computer key, and the amount of statistical data that the individual can easily access is virtually unlimited. Unfortunately, none of these developments does anything to improve the individual investor's odds in the stock market. Indeed, today's rapid proliferation of investment data and quicker access to this data more often than not tend to shift the market participants from being long-term fundamental investors to becoming short-term, technically oriented traders, and it is this psychological shift from investing to speculating that will prove to be the undoing of today's investment mania.

It has long been said that while history never repeats itself, it often rhymes, and the rhythm of the stock market is inviolate. As the cumulative thoughts of its millions of participants, the stock market is nothing more than a psychological reflection of the investing public's changing levels of optimism and pessimism. Stock valuations can move hundreds of percentage points from bear market lows to bull market highs. These swings are much wider than the actual change in the real value of the underlying shares. But while real value may remain relatively unchanged, there are changes in the parameters that apply to the market's value, parameters that are set based on the public's level of fear and greed. In long-running bull periods, stocks rise to levels that are higher than warranted by their fundamentals.

Likewise, in bearish phases, the parameters fall to levels that are equally unwarranted on the downside. As simple as it sounds, long-term success in the stock market is little more than knowing where one stands in relation to these cycles and buying and selling accordingly. Those who invest in sync with these long-term cycles cannot lose, while those who ignore the psychological underpinnings of the investment world are doomed to eventual failure.

John Templeton noted that the human emotion factor is the single most important aspect of the stock market. In fact, he says, "it is only by understanding the emotions of others that an investor has a chance to produce superior results."

Before we look at the current state of the market, let's first look at the psychological characteristics that make up a successful investor and isolate those qualities that have separated the few from the many. Indeed, after 15 years of studying the market and its participants, I have found that successful investors, those who are able to compile successful track records through many market cycles, share several common traits.

First and foremost, as in most pursuits, the development of any successful market approach requires that investors know themselves and be psychologically comfortable with their chosen investment strategy. Their is no one correct investment approach. Each person comes to the investment arena with his or her own background, values, goals, and degrees of emotional control, all of which must be in tune with the particular market approach that is used. To fail to be psychologically comfortable with a chosen investment strategy is like running a race in someone else's track shoes, not a good plan for an investor who wants to win.

Some by nature will be able to handle the greater risks involved in buying stocks that rank highest in relative strength. Others are comfortable picking out seemingly unfavorable bargains. Templeton had long been comfortable scouring the globe for unknown stocks that might prosper over the subsequent decade. Peter Lynch was more comfortable looking at household names at the local mall. Michael Price was comfortable looking for value among bankrupt companies. Investment styles ebb and flow, and each of these approaches will sometimes be favored with the market's primary trend and sometimes not. But most importantly, these long-term successful investors maintain their investment approach throughout. Their goal is above-average returns with below-average risk over full market cycles. They don't let the market dictate their approach. A person's ability to accurately appraise his or her own psychological makeup and then to use that information to guide market strategy is an essential building block for any successful investor. It is important that investors have a narrow focus and avoid the need to know everything, while concentrating only on what they know best.

Warren Buffett one said, "As an investor, you must stick within your circle of competence." You have to know what you understand and what you don't understand. It's not terribly important how big that circle of competence is, but it is terribly important that you know where the perimeter is.

You can be successful in the stock market and know nothing about moving averages, oscillators, program trading, support, and resistance lines. You need not follow every stock group listed by Standard & Poor's. In the stock market, quantity is no replacement for quality. What separates investing in stocks from rolling the dice at a gambling table is the ability in the stock market to make rational long-term judgments. In the stock market, you can isolate specific trends, make an assessment of the future prospects of a product or a service or a concept. It's a game of intelligence in which you pit your knowledge and common sense against others, and if your long-term analysis is correct, you win. By limiting your focus, you will also be able to take concentrated positions that mean something in dollars and cents.

Diversification may have its benefits for smaller or less sophisticated investors, but investment greatness only comes to those who are willing to go out on the limb in a meaningful way. John Maynard Keynes wrote, "It's a mistake to think that one can limit one's risk by spreading their money among many enterprises about which they know little. Personally, there are seldom more than two or three investments at any one time in which I'm willing to put my full confidence." If you are an investor who is well-versed in a particular company and its markets, you will have a much better chance of understanding the effects of economic and corporate news that can impact that holding. If you're confident in a company's long-range prospects, it becomes easier to add to positions during price setbacks.

Meanwhile, always be willing to be wrong. Given that every market transaction represents one seller and one buyer, every time a transaction is made, somebody made a mistake. Mistakes are part of the game.

And every market player at one time or another will make a mistake. But understanding your losses may prove the most valuable step toward success. Everyone makes mistakes; but what separates the best from the rest is that when they do make a mistake, they accept it, they analyze it, they learn from it, and then they move on. They don't take it personally, Remember, the stock doesn't know you own it.

As a corollary, it is essential to avoid big losses. As one Indy 500 winner once said, "To finish first, you must first finish." As obvious as this sounds, the sad truth is that few investors take action to prevent a big loss. It's a function of greed. Most people, when they buy something, are thinking only about how much money they are going to make instead of how much money they're willing to lose. In good markets, that's okay; but in down or sideways markets, many investors end up sitting with one or two paper losses—big losses—waiting to get even. What it gets down to is preservation of capital. They can't play the game when they lose their chips.

Perhaps most important is the need to keep things simple. The biggest mistake made in the investment world by most individuals is that they tend to make the investment process more difficult than it needs to be. Don't bother looking for foolproof systems. None of the investment greats has made his or her reputation on derivatives, options, currencies, or futures. None operates with 900 numbers or hotlines, and while many incorporate some basic technical analysis into their overall strategies, none is strictly a technician.

No consistently successful investor has replaced investment intelligence with computer programs. Indeed, Warren Buffett has said that investment intelligence has gone backward over the past 40 years. To quote Buffett, "Too many investors substitute analysis for common sense. In this field, we see a great averaging of IQs in a largely offsetting fashion, but we think that's nonsense." Why this fascination for figures? Buffett explains, "It's simple. It's a function of the academic background of many of today's young market participants who are so well-versed in higher mathematics and computer skills. Every MBA loves to run a million statistical comparisons of one variable versus another for, as the saying goes, to a man with a hammer, every problem looks like a nail."

The week after John Templeton retired, I was lucky enough to visit with him at his home and to spend a couple of hours as he reflected on his 60-year career. Before leaving, I asked him what he felt was the single most important advice he could give an investor. His response, "Ignore the market. Don't even try to guess its direction. Buy quality stocks at undervalued prices, and just hold on until those values are recognized." It doesn't get any simpler than that.

The most important factor to allow you to let the market's underlying simplicity shine through is to understand the importance of viewing stocks as operating businesses. Speculators view stocks as pieces of paper that are purchased for the sake of finding someone else at a future time willing to pay more. An investor, on the other hand, buys a stock to benefit from owning a stake in a business. Lynch notes that his biggest profits always came during the third, fourth, or fifth year of owning a stock. Buffett views stock ownership in the same manner as buying the entire company. If he wouldn't want to own the entire business, he isn't interested in participating in any of its shares.

Speculators, on the other hand, benefit from the "greater fool" theory of investing. Seen today in the form of momentum investing, the theory is that a stock's absolute value is irrelevant. The purpose

163

of owning the stock is simply because it is expected that someone will pay a more foolish price at a later date. This approach is fine as long as the momentum is toward higher prices and rising overall valuations. But just like musical chairs, someone eventually gets left without a chair. At some point, the number of greater fools willing to buy momentum stocks at increasingly overvalued prices will dwindle.

Importantly, if you view stocks as businesses, your investment horizon by necessity will become long-term. This ability to focus on the long term, more than anything else, is what will position an investor for eventual success. In today's world of instant communication, there are many forces at work trying to separate them from their holdings. In requires discipline to hold on.

The most difficult force to withstand is today's all-knowing media. Investors are deluged with news and opinions on the meaning of that news, almost as soon as it happens. They hear about it on TV, read about it in their newspapers, and learn about it from their brokers. But being instantly and totally informed about their stocks often forces long-term investors to make too many emotional decisions, one of which is likely to be wrong. Remember, long-established trends are not easily reversed. Most news, as sensational as it may sound at the time, does not involve basic fundamental change. It simply is not as bad or as good as it sounds at the time the news is released. News in the media strive for immediacy. The goal is to instantly inform, but it is the passage of time that puts news into its proper perspective.

As Warren Buffett so aptly points out, "You can't produce a baby in one month by getting nine women pregnant." Indeed, the ability to focus on long-term growth of quality businesses via the stock market is a major advantage enjoyed by individuals over the institutional crowd. With so many money managers being judged on a quarterly basis, the need to perform on a par with one's peers over the short term is overwhelming. Unfortunately, to avoid the chance of underperformance, many institutional investors will act in sync. No one gets fired for buying the same stock that everyone else is buying. Conformity becomes a safety net, but outperformance will only come to those who avoid this mentality.

Bernard Baruch was a man of few words, and when asked the most important lesson he had learned in a lifetime of investing, his simple response was, "Never follow the crowd." It may sound cynical, but in the long run, the crowd will always be wrong. If you only buy stocks when they are extremely popular, you'll invariably be buying toward the top. Going against the crowd is extremely difficult to do, but in the long run it is the most likely approach to success.

Templeton notes, "Simple common sense tells you that the lowest price for an asset can occur only when the maximum number of owners are pessimistic." It has to be that way; it can be no other. If 10 doctors tell you to take a certain medicine, you'd be wise to take it. If 10 civil engineers tell you to build a bridge a certain way, then you should build it that way. But in selecting securities, consensus is dangerous. Adds Templeton, "If ten security analysts tell you to buy a certain asset, stay away. That popularity must be already reflected in a high price."

This market in recent years has gone further and higher than most could have ever envisioned. But this really shouldn't come as a surprise because once a trend becomes well-established on Wall Street, it always goes on to unexpected extremes. It's exceedingly difficult to reverse. Market history is replete with these examples. The love affair with gold stocks in the sixties, the obsession with the "nifty-fifty" growth stocks in the seventies, and the boom in debt, junk, and Pacific Rim investing in the eighties all represented trends characterized by unexpected heights and sustainability. Today we are seeing a similar trend in technology. There are few people as bullish on the technological advances of modern society as I am—advances in computers and communications, and more recently developments concerning the Internet, are truly awe inspiring. But don't confuse a good concept with a good investment value. If you foresaw the potential of automobiles in the 1920s, you could have invested in over 200 publicly traded auto stocks. Unfortunately, only three survived. Everyone could see the potential of biotechnology in the late seventies and early eighties, but few envisioned that eight of ten publicly traded firms at that time would cease to exist by the end of the decade. In the late 1960s, any stock that mentioned its role in electronics was sure to outperform.

In 1968, Ben Graham conducted a study of the 48 electronic companies that were then listed in Standard & Poor's. Three years later, 23 of the 45 had declined in price by more than 15 percent; 12 were dropped from the list completely; and only 2 of the 45 electronic stocks had actually risen over the subsequent three years. How many of the scores of publicly traded personal computer makers from the early 1980s are still here today? Less than a handful. And how many of today's Internet pioneers are likely to be the long-term winners a few years from now? Only time will tell, but in today's high-tech stock arena, "buyer beware" is more appropriate advice than ever.

The stock market's most overriding trend today is the shift of household and retirement assets from savings accounts and other conservative investment vehicles into the higher-risk stock market. From 1982 through the early 1990s, I urged readers of my publications to own stocks. It was a hard sell, despite the many compelling arguments in favor of stock ownership as historically undervalued prices for much of the decade. Few individuals had any interest in owning stocks. They were perceived as a high-risk venture. But it was the market's out-of-favor status that made the accumulation of stocks since the early eighties a generally successful proposition. But stocks are no longer seen as risky. The argument to buy stocks is no longer a hard sell. Indeed, virtually all individuals now see the stock market as a sure path to double-digit annual gains.

Ironically, the hard sell now, and my message after a decade of rampant bullishness, is the need for caution and a more open-minded understanding of risk. Indeed, there is one characteristic in today's market that I find particularly alarming: the overwhelming lack of sophistication of many of today's individual market players, as well as many of its professionals. In a recent poll of Vanguard fund holders on their knowledge of mutual funds, only 16 percent of the respondents received a passing score. One-third believed that government securities were guaranteed not to lose money. Over a third believed that mutual fund diversification eliminated the risk of losing their funds—not reduced their risk, but *eliminated* it. An *Investor's Daily* poll of investors over age 65 showed that nearly half believed that mutual funds were protected against loss by the Federal Deposit Insurance Corporation. They're not.

At 37 years old, I am an old-timer in this business. Recent estimates show that the average age of today's mutual fund managers is 30 and that their average tenure in the investment field is 3.7 years. Only one in seven mutual fund managers has ever seen a bear market, and fewer than one in five was a market participant in 1987. To many young fund managers with whom I speak and who handle multibillion dollar portfolios of other people's money, investing is a game. Many of them readily admit that they have little understanding of the specific stocks they buy, and they often don't know even the basic fundamental facts concerning these issues. Those who buy for the wrong reasons will eventually get the wrong results.

Meanwhile, the vast majority of individuals who hold these equity funds are similarly inexperienced in downside risk. The last time that the stock market underwent a 10 percent decline was 1990. Since then, assets in equity funds have grown from $226 billion to $1.3 trillion. In other words, $4.17 of every $5.00 now invested in the stock market has never ridden through even a minor market correction. More money has gone into stock funds in the past 5 years than in the prior 66 years, and mutual fund assets, as of mid-1996, exceed national savings. In other words, the money now in the stock market represents the lion's share of middle-class America's savings, and this is occurring after 14 years of rising prices, with the stock market now trading at its most overvalued fundamental level in history. And few of these investors realize that there is any risk surrounding their nesteggs.

There are many other signs of speculative excess. The Supplemental Benefits Program of Alaska, that state's version of Social Security, has just agreed to allow the equity exposure of many of its participants to be raised to 90 percent. National lawmakers are seeking to allow Social Security funds to be invested in stock to boost long-term returns. And the message to buy stocks is seen everywhere. A popular science fiction book club is now soliciting its members to buy the best 100 stocks in America. One 1996 issue of *Time Magazine* had 18 full pages of personal finance ads. It has always been a sign of caution when the number of bullish ads in *Barron's* significantly exceeded the number of bearish ads. Through recent months, however, there have been no bearish ads.

Playboy magazine is now releasing its rankings of mutual funds. *Consumer Reports* has added mutual funds to its consumer coverage, and *Cosmopolitan* magazine profiled CNBC's David Farber as its new stock market hunk. Scores of mutual funds are now advertising directly to consumers, and the logo of choice for this homespun message is none other than the family dog. Fidelity's latest ads feature a dog staring at an empty bowl. Scudder's ads have a dog with an envelope in its mouth. Janus's ads have a dog chasing its tail. But by far my favorite is a TV ad where a little boy gets shares of a mutual fund for his birthday instead of toys and exclaims, "Wow! It's just what I've always wanted." If that's not enough, you can now send your nine-year-old to stock market camp at the Ritz Carlton in Palm Beach; the campers are given financial planning courses and are driven by limousine to Worth Avenue brokerage firms.

In 1992, there were less than 1,000 investment clubs. In 1995, that number had quintupled to 5,000; and by 1996 that number has again quadrupled to over 21,000. One of these clubs is run by the Beardstown Ladies, who now have two best-selling books promoting 34 percent safe annual returns from a buy-and-hold strategy. The motley fools who operate the popular online site on America On-Line began their web site before they were 30 years old with no knowledge whatsoever, nor experience, nor insight into the stock market. Yet they confidently extrapolated the past into the future, allowing them to predict to tens of thousands of online followers, "We're moving Coca-Cola to $225 a share by 2005, rise in the Gap to $200, Microsoft to $1,200 a share, and Nike to $750. All forecasts calling for 20 to 30 percent returns over each and every year for the next decade."

The *Wall Street Money Machine* is a new best seller that was written by a cab driver, and almost unbelievably, another new best seller called *The Whiz Kid of Wall Street's Investment Guide* was just written by a teenager. Clearly the desire of the public to believe that stocks offer a guaranteed road to riches has reached a new level of popularity. And while none of these new market gurus believe that one needs to look back at history in assessing the market's future, I would caution you that this mania is not a first-time event. Indeed, a mutual fund mania has occurred in every generation in this century. It was seen in the mania for investment trusts in the 1920s and 1930s. The next generational move into funds occurred in the 1960s, the famed era of contractual investment plans and go-go funds. And finally, we are now seeing another move in the 1990s.

John Kenneth Galbraith, in his *Short History of Financial Euphoria*, isolated the four trends that signify an investment mania. The first is that investors lose sight of risk and focus only on the rewards. The second is a belief that there are new circumstances in the world that justify higher-than-normal valuations. The third is the illusion that despite temporary setbacks, values are certain to continue rising. And the fourth is condemnation of those who express doubt or dissent to the currently bullish view. Needless to say, all four of these signs are widely prevalent in today's environment.

How, then, do I reconcile my bullish belief to buy quality stocks and focus on the long-term prospects of the underlying companies with my extremely negative assessment of the current state of the market? Easy. View this not as a stock market but strictly as a market of individual stocks. In every market environment there are good stocks trading at good values. Isolating that value may be more difficult today than in the past, but it is not impossible.

Here are some guidelines. First and foremost, be prepared and accept an eventual sell-off, perhaps a very significant sell-off, in the overall stock market. Those who are likely to sell out on market weakness should begin doing so now while stocks remain in a rising trend. Meanwhile, the truly long-term investor should make sure that they are psychologically prepared to hold on through interim weakness and to use those setbacks to add to well-thought-out long-term positions. Don't let fear and weakness turn you, a long-term investor, into a short-term seller.

Most importantly, this is a time to shift assets out of stocks that are already the favorites among institutions. The same mentality that has driven favored market sectors to unsustainably high levels will eventually result in a mass exodus from these same positions. Leaving a portfolio sitting in the path of the herd may result in irreparable damage.

Diversify internationally. While a major setback in domestic issues will likely affect markets around the globe, you'll greatly reduce the overall risk of a portfolio by holding value-oriented positions in other markets. Focus on market sectors that have not fully participated in this market's run to new highs. Look at natural resources, look at utilities, look at real estate investment trusts, look at stock with solid fundamentals and a long history of dividend payments, rather than at the latest favored momentum plays. And, most of all, in my opinion, look at smaller cap growth stocks that are typically too illiquid to attract the attention of large institutions. Indeed, it is this sector that I believe offers the most exciting long-term growth situations with the least amount of market risk in today's environment.

Despite the market's general overvaluation, I continue to find exciting long-term growth opportunities that are as yet unrecognized on Wall Street, either because they are temporarily out of favor because they don't show up on momentum-based computer screens or because, due to special situations, they require a fundamental outlook and a willingness to go against the crowd. Yet, these are the situations in which you can find real value today.

It is important to maintain much higher than average cash levels so that when others are selling and abandoning, you can be there scooping up great long-term bargains. Be patient and avoid the feeling that you must jump on the already-crowded bandwagon. Patience applies not only to holding on to the stocks you already own, but also to waiting for the opportune time to initiate or to add to one's positions. So take it slow, and don't get caught up in unrealistic expectations.

Sell overvalued holdings, raise some extra cash, focus temporarily on preservation of capital, and be patient. Today's investment mania will pass, as it has before, in the natural rhythm of the stock market.

CHAPTER 11

The Stock Market Hysteria Still to Come

Basil Chapman

The Mega Bull Market

"Stock tickers at McDonald's? Record-high sculptured skyscrapers? 250-mile-per-hour (mph) luxurious grand-touring cars? 4,000-passenger 'ocean cities' to nowhere? As the supercharged Dow accelerates to ever-increasing record highs, most of the socioeconomic parallels of the mid-1920s point to a 'megamove' in the Dow just beginning to unfold. The seeds of a surge into the decade of the mega trends have already been sown."
—Chapman Marketline, Summer 1988

A COUNTRY CONSUMED WITH THE STOCK MARKET

In the 1990s, as the stock market eventually powers to record high after record high, the number of individuals participating in the stock market will reach unprecedented levels. Buying will become so pervasive that even a McDonald's in a remote area will feel the need to feed diners quotes with their meals. Individual stocks will swing 10 to

12 points in a session. The public, loath to miss a beat, will want to watch their latest bets/investments grow by the minute.

In the 1920s the advent of the glass-domed ticker gave the public an opportunity to constantly monitor their portfolios. For us in the 1990s, quotes will be everywhere, all the time: on computers, televisions, and storefront windows. Eventually, the stock market will collapse, just as the international "Tulip Bulb" mania of the early 1600s led to a collapse when the cost of bulbs reached the prices of houses.

THE HEIGHTS OF BUILDINGS RISE COMMENSURATE WITH THE STOCK MARKET

The skyscraper phenomenon refers to the way each new generation of skyscrapers demands cutting-edge technology (Otis developed a new elevator system in the 1920s, soon after used for the extended height of the Empire State Building). A marvel of design and engineering ingenuity, skyscrapers require such a huge scale of financial, technological and logistical resources that it is obvious why they become the last extravagance of a mega bull market cycle. Finally they become "affordable." Not needed in any functional way, the tallest skyscraper rather becomes a fitting coda and a state-of-the-art time-freeze of wealth and technology.

SIZE INCREASES AS A "BIGGER IS BETTER" PHASE UNFOLDS

Cruise ships, impossible to fund during recessionary times, invariably appear as the economy improves and vacationers feel comfortable enough to treat themselves to something different. The cruise ships being built, or in the planning stages, are so huge that they resemble "ocean cities" (*Chapman Marketline*, August 1985). With every conceivable amenity on board, they will accommodate thousands of vacationers, and of course, like the luxury liners of the 1920s, they too will have brokerage offices aboard. This is also the period during which immense projects such as the longest bridge in the world or the building of new rail systems or airports are begun. Interestingly, these huge projects invariably overlap into the "bad" times, ready to give employment to thousands who would otherwise not have jobs. (The George Washington Bridge and the Manhattan Train System began construction and overhauling, respectively, in the 1020s and ended in the 1930s.)

A FINAL, LUXURIOUS, EXTRAVAGANT PHASE

In the late 1920s and early 1930s there were incredibly expensive, fast, and luxurious Duesenbergs, Bentleys and Cadillacs. We are not yet there. But we are on our way to 250 mph grand-touring cars purchased with high profits from the stock market.

TALL BUILDINGS AND THE (APPROXIMATELY) 37-YEAR ECONOMIC CYCLE

For over 100 years, construction of the tallest buildings in the world has concluded economic booms. Culminating a deflationary period, tall buildings were designed as the stock market was peaking in 1891 and then completed during the stock market panic of 1893 and the silver collapse in 1895. The first of three approximately 37-year economic surges resulted in skyscrapers: Chicago's Home Insurance Building in 1885, the Reliance Building in 1894, and New York's (still spectacular) Flatiron Building in 1902.

The roaring 'twenties saw the construction of the famous Rockefeller Center, followed by the beautiful Chrysler Building. The Chrysler Building, completed in 1930, was not only designed to be the tallest building—made so by the surreptitious last-hour raising of an extension spike just two feet above the previous record height—but was styled after the 1929 hood ornament. Capping that era and within weeks of the Dow Jones Industrial Average's final Labor-Day-weekend 1929 high at 381, papers were signed to begin work on the Empire State

Building. Just eight weeks later the Dow was under 200. The soon-to-be-nicknamed Empty State Building opened on May 1, 1931; the Dow was at 56.

The second 37-year cycle came with the 1960s economic surge (led by the nifty fifty stocks), as the Dow double-topped around the 1000 mark. Epitomizing that growth period, shiny metal and glass-clad skyscrapers were built (e.g., Boston's John Hancock Tower, planned in the late 1960s and completed in the 1970s). Detroit's fintailed behemoths with monster front grills getting only 10 miles per gallon of gas culminated that era of excessive consumption. (Today, sport utility vehicles (SUVs) are becoming almost unmanageably huge; and if recent report are correct, these vehicles are scheduled to become much larger and more luxurious by the century's turn. That will be at least a warning sign. It completely ignores the question of another oil crisis.)

Today, with the skyscrapers being built in Asia, we are again seeing an economic boom reflected in the height of buildings. This phenomenon has not yet arrived here in the United States, however it is only a matter of time before we too get swept up in the competition to build the world's tallest building.

Interestingly, moving 37 years forward from the 1966 cap on the Dow at 1000 takes us to approximately the 2001 to 2003 time frame: the major peak in this mega bull cycle. A hint of the coming market top in the United States could well be the collapse of Malaysia's tremendous economic boom just months after the Petronas Towers in Kuala Lumpur, the world's tallest buildings, were completed.

That economic collapse triggered sell-offs in other Asian markets, in October 1997, which the media quickly labeled "the Asian meltdown."

THE STOCK MARKET MEASURES OUR ACTIONS, WHILE THE MEDIA MEASURE OUR REACTIONS

As Asian stock markets crumbled in overnight trading, news reporters and camera crews were stationed at trading desks and outside brokerage houses around the United States the following day. They were preparing to interview investors for great human stories of heartbreak and despair.

Investors awoke on October 28, 1997, to an avalanche of negative Asian economic news. The media devoted an inordinate amount of space and time to interviews from experts around the world. (Many were the same "experts" who recommended the Asian countries as investments just months before.) As expected, the Down opened sharply lower that day, cascading some 190 points. And then, to the surprise—and probably the disappointment—of the news media, a funny thing happened—a *selling climax*. Within an hour-and-a-half the Dow had reversed, and on record-breaking volume it closed up 337 points on the day! A whopping 500-plus point reversal. Simply put: there were no sellers left.

This media-frenzied international crisis was a market turning point. When an international news story is small-town conversation, that is often a major market indicator. The media's handwringing turns into a seminal market event.

HEADLINES AS A REVERSAL TECHNIQUE

Attempting to identify major market lows and highs is difficult, but occasionally warning signs flash very clearly, like October 28, 1997. Investors often throw away their losing stocks in disgust or fear right at market bottoms or buy in at market tops. Most buying or selling climaxes occur when the tone and the volume of either negative or positive information accelerates to a crescendo of banner headlines, thereby exacerbating an irrational response from investors. As newspaper headline size increases with the seriousness of the issue involved and the duration between news reports shortens, perspective is difficult to maintain. Investors suddenly feel they must "do something." As they are swept along, a herd mentality prevails and good judgment takes a back seat. Often the final result is diametrically opposite to the prevailing opinion just hours earlier.

On January 16, 1991, when war was declared against Iraq, the stock market had already dropped significantly in anticipation of the conflict as market indicators achieved their highest oversold reading ever. *Headlines screamed negativism. But* on Thursday, January 17, the Dow opened almost 100 points up and then closed even higher, initiating an entirely new up phase.

SOCIOECONOMIC, SENTIMENT, AND TECHNICAL INDICATORS ON THE MACRO LEVEL

Short-term or long-term the market goes from overbought to oversold. Whether looking at the macro overview (100 years or more) or analyzing the micro shorter-term perspective (minutes), the one element that remains constant is human nature.

Gloom and doom were pervasive in the early 1980s. With yet another recession under way economic reports in the spring and summer of 1982 were filled with the latest round of bad earnings reports and inflationary prices. Interest rates were at exceptionally high levels and there was unrelentingly negative news on the economy and inflation (newspapers and talk shows commiserating over the end of America as we've know it). But under this bearish sentiment, the stock market's technical condition showed really positive systemic changes taking place. The market's descent leveled out and turned upward that summer.

FRUGALITY TO COMPLACENCY TO EXCESSIVITY

A period similar to that of the Harding-Coolidge-Hoover era was likely to unfold. All the ingredients were there: potential tax cuts, budget balancing, trade surplus even with trade barriers, deflation, political scandal (Teapot Dome), unemployment lows, peace treaties, much lower interest rates, the return of jazz as a popular art form, money was being raised to refurbish the popular landmarks of the 1890s and 1920s, a turn from the austere toward consumerism, and son on. "The frugal, ascetic, and serious 1970s could eventually become the gluttonous, fun-loving, and frivolous 1990s" (*Chapman Marketline*, early 1984).

LOWER INTEREST RATES: THE FUEL FOR AN EXTENDED BULL MOVE IN STOCKS

For an extended period of economic growth, interest rates must decline sharply. In the summer of 1983 there was a veritable advertising blitz by banks touting their latest high interest payments on savings accounts and certificates of deposit. That type of blatant competition is usually the first warning sign of a pending trend change. Also, numerous technical indicators helped confirm a "sell" signal on the Treasury-bond (T-bond) yield (*Chapman Marketline*, August 1983). Using the pendulum analogy plus trendline analysis, a very long term target in the 5 percent or lower area for T-bond yields appeared likely. While rates declined, the axiom "lower yields equals higher stock prices" would remain in force. Later, if rates were still reasonably low, the Dow would be powered parabolically higher into the five digits *on sheer buying hysteria.*

RIGHT, BUT WRONG

When the stock market crashed in 1987, it took the Dow much lower than anticipated from that summer's August sell signal (*Chapman Marketline*, August, 1987). Significantly, the signs of major excesses that should accompany a pending major top were not yet evident. Rather, the positive economic changes identified back in the early to mid-1980s were still unfolding on schedule. That implied that another major up phase of the mega bull market was about to begin (*Chapman Marketline*, Oct. 20, 1987). In 1988 and 1989, the socioeconomic structure of the mega bull market appeared very strong. With interest rates on the decline and commodities pointing downward, it confirmed that the long-term target of a 5 percent (or better) yield was still on track. Other parabolic chart patterns overlaid on the Dow's chart pointed to a high probability of the 7900 level being achieved in 1997—possibly even higher. That coincided with the bigger socioeconomic picture pointing to a final top coming in 1997—if the British returning Hong Kong to the Chinese in that year triggered an international sell-off (*Chapman Marketline*, 1988).

Looking at the socioeconomic picture in July 1988, there were only hints at the type of icons mentioned in the opening paragraph, that is, skyscrapers and luxurious grand touring cars. That forecast of a major top in 1997 was immediately extended out even further, possibly to the century's end with the Dow skyrocketing into the 12,500 to 15,000 area. Significantly, as those forecasts from the mid-1980s of low interest rates, surprisingly low unemployment, and strong signs of the expected budget surplus going into the black have unfolded, the ultimate high continued to be raised even higher.

The sideways consolidation of 1994 essentially set the stage for "rolling" corrections to become the characteristic of the next phase of the mega bull market. (That is were overbought sectors decline sharply at different times, thus maintaining a much higher closing price in the Dow and the Standard & Poor's (S&P) 500 Index than in a classic bear market collapse, in which everything cascades down together.

What is evident in this 1997 period is that we have the potential to copy the action of the Japanese Nikkei Dow in 1987. When the 1987 DJIA crash occurred, the Nikkei was impacted far less, declining about 12 to 13 percent. And then, within six months, the Nikkei was breaking out to new all-time highs. The Dow Jones Industrials' response has so far (since the October 28 low) matched the Nikkei's pattern in 1987. That is a very encouraging sign.

PUSHING AWAY FROM A LONG PERIOD OF UNCERTAINTY INTO A PERIOD OF COMPLACENCY

The tumultuous years from 1915 to 1919 saw conscription, war, and finally an influenza epidemic that claimed over half a million lives. The economy slumped in 1920 and 1921 as the Dow plummeted to the 65 area. The return of peace and prosperity was a welcome relief. That stability and continuing economic growth led to a period of complacency (while far more extended in time and price, the years from 1986 until the present have been remarkably similar to the 1923–1927 period). Also, this period of tame inflation and peace is in stark contrast to the inflationary and inflammatory 1970s.

After the complacency of the mid-1920s, an era of excessiveness evolved, culminating in the heady days of the roaring 'twenties. A telling symbol of that exuberance was that after three years of increasing demand and with great fanfare, Rolls Royce presented their newest and most powerful model on October 29, 1929. A fitting contrary indicator and the consummate irony, the most expensive Rolls ever was displayed in the *New York Times*, directly opposite the stock tables of the previous session's closing prices. That followed one of the worst days during the crash. Worse, it was only four days after "Black Thursday." Now that's market timing!

STRUCTURAL CHANGE MUST ACCOMPANY A BULL MARKET FOR SUSTAINABILITY

During the industrial malaise of the late 1970s and the early 1980s, *Consumer Reports* gave virtually all U.S.-made cars the absolute worst ratings while Americans embraced Japanese automobiles and electronic goods for their superior workmanship. That competition forced our automobile industry to go from cost-cutting inefficiencies and shoddy workmanship to quality, pride, and innovation. "If my prognosis of good economic times ahead is correct, then General Motors will once again become the premier auto company, with Cadillac returning as the national symbol of success" (*Chapman Marketline*, 1985).

The following year Americans rushed to buy Japanese-made cars—even as the yen was pushing to record levels. "Ironically, as our dollar begins to soar higher and higher in the late 1990s, so too will our trade exports rise to record levels. More significantly, for the first time in decades the label 'Made in the USA' will become much sought

179

after as a status symbol not just here, *but especially abroad*" (*Chapman Marketline*, Fall 1986).

REAL ESTATE AS AN INFLATION HEDGE

"To fight inflation one must own an increasing asset like real estate." That was the mantra of the early 1980s. After all, property ownership enabled one to "come out ahead," Ironically, real estate's attractiveness in the final phase of the mega bull cycle will be negatively impacted by lower interest rates. The stock market's rise will usurp much of the funds usually allocated to real estate. Capital appreciation from the stock market has far outpaced real estate since the 1987 crash. And that should continue except at the highest end of the luxury home and posh vacation home sector. In the 1926-to-1929 period, the average price of a house actually declined in value. Unfortunately it takes the public many years to let go of a belief imbedded into the cumulative psyche, at which point the "new" belief is probably as untimely as the "old" one. Just reflect on the general mood during the bank crisis and the layoffs of the early 1990s, or on the incessant talk about a budget deficit. Now there is the Social Security scare. In each of the earlier cases the problem was resolved in the market place as the headlines were increasing on the front pages.

It was with inflationary expectations that the public in the Northeast resorted to bidding wars for houses and other properties in 1983. Danger signs began to show up in 1984. All indications pointed to a major top looming on the horizon for the real estate market. Declining interest rates were very bullish for stocks. Many big-cap stocks hadn't even broken out from their long-term bases. In piecing together the parts of the economic jigsaw, it appeared that when the real estate market eventually did peak, it would leave just one "commodity" to have its parabolic upsurge in the latter part of the twentieth century: *stocks.*

In the spring of 1985 Boston-area rental property had risen to a level where it was difficult, if not impossible, to find a multifamily dwelling that had any cash flow after expenses. Extremely high prices of rental homes made for substantial monthly payments as expenses overwhelmed receipts. Nonetheless, rental home owners seemed convinced that large profits when selling their properties would more than make up any shorter term deficits. *Unfortunately, when reality and dreams part company for too long, reality usually wins.*

The *Boston Globe* devoted a special article in the real estate section of its Sunday paper to the benefits of owning rental property early in the summer of 1985. Contrary opinion plus the tremendous surge in prices indicated that the rental housing sector was becoming frothy. The following year, as prices were still rising sharply, another article in the *Boston Globe* focused on the benefits of owning a vacation home on Cape Cod. Prices there escalated. Another warning sign was the steadily increasing numbers of "No money down" real estate investment "shows" and seminars. That quickly became an avalanche. In 1986 a "sell" on real estate was given. Although a year too early, the 1987 stock market crash rapidly burst that real estate bubble. Today, most properties are still far under those heady peak levels.

At the time of that mid-1980s sell on real estate, a distinction was made. While the broader real estate market would seriously lag the stock market, top-quality property (huge estates with swimming pools, tennis courts, and quarters for guests, maids, and chauffeurs), downtown office buildings, and very specific situations and sites especially related to mega projects would continue to do very well in the 1990s. As stocks outpaced real estate, the bull market would usurp the bulk of investment monies. Renting would become popular again as potential home owners decided that the gains in the stock market increased more rapidly than the value of their home. In the period 1926 through 1929 the average home lost money while the stock market more than doubled (having gone from the 160s to the 380s on the Dow Average).

LEGISLATION: THE CABOOSE

In late 1987, the "from bricks to paper" theme began unfolding (*Chapman Marketline*, 1986). Equity built up over many decades by investors in the real estate market would eventually be moved into the stock market.

Legislation invariably favors a bullish area on the way up and turns bearish on the way down. The direction becomes an issue after it is clearly identifiable to the public and close to evaporating. That is when politicians step in to do their civic duty, to fix the problem, at the point of greatest ineffectualism. Whichever way, it is invariably too much, too late. By then the real issue has become virtually nonexistent. Even worse, a countertrend directional move has already begun. In the end, history gets legislated, not the present or the future (which was the original intent), thus creating a problem for the future. Were there tax cuts in the tough 1970s? No! But now that the stock market has provided exceptional returns for years and the economy is booming, there is even talk of capital gains being completely eliminated.

Over the past decade we have seen an increasing desire by politicians to target the real estate market with potentially negative legislation. Whether it be through tax disincentives (increasing the depreciation time table), or through potential changes in the way real estate investment trusts (REITs), rentals, or other real estate vehicles are treated for tax purposes, the favorable focus evident in the 1980s would change. Consequently, laws favoring real estate as an investment will become less desirable, while in counterpoint, stock ownership will be stimulated through legislative encouragement.

Legislators have waited patiently in the caboose until now. They have checked the direction of the billowing smoke and are very carefully moving up to the front of the train. Watch out, real estate. The politicians are coming toward the engine to stoke the stock market.

FASHION IS THE GREAT DICTATOR OF TRENDS

This mega bull market will remain unstoppable until the last penny has been wrung from the public. The investing public is now global. As the Dow pushes ever higher, foreigners will see the United States as the safest place on earth to invest, thereby fueling the stock market even more. When the Japanese Nikkei was soaring into the 30,000s, money poured into the Japanese market. The belief was that the Japanese had a perfect economic system. American businesses studied their formula, as "emulation" became the theme. But at the height of their glory, as the Nikkei was lunging toward 39,000, the rug was pulled from under them. (*Chapman Marketline*, April 1979, "target 39,000 for a major peak in the Nikkei—a top that could last some 30 to 40 years. Simultaneously, the DJIA/dollar should trade places with the Nikkei/yen as they pass one another in opposite directions over the coming years.")

As mentioned earlier, the fashion now is to invest in the stock market. No amount of dissuasion will change that. What took the general public over 15 years to understand cannot be changed until the last believer is won over.

BANKS AS CONTRARY INDICATORS

Even when badly needed in the late 1920s, bank regulations were lax. Instituted with President Roosevelt in the early 1930s, they were useless when no one had any money. Theoretically, tighter bank regulations are needed now. Instead, like the late 1920s, regulations are being lifted or eased; Roosevelt's regulations are being tossed out.

The historical safeguards that would elongate this mega bull market, such s not allowing banks in any way to be involved with stocks except in the typical fiduciary tradition or limiting their buying of brokerage houses, are all crumbling. The banking industry has a penchant for getting into a trend when it is practically over: bonds, real estate, and now stocks.

The real estate crash of 1987 showed once again banks' poor timing as mortgage activity dried up and banks across the country closed or were shut down. (As a contrary indicator though, one recalls the gory headlines when beaten-down bank stocks were trading in the single digits in the early 1990s. Now they are recording banner headlines as many are pushing into the triple digits.) One of the focal points of the "Trendswatch" section back in the mid-1980s was (and remains) that banks and brokerage houses would gobble one another up, and "conglomerates" would return as the economy demanded a larger scale, especially for international business. So, as the antithesis of the "lean and mean" era of the 1980s, the slogan would become "bigger is better."

FROM SAFE INVESTMENTS TO
MORE SPECULATIVE AREAS

"As the bull market becomes the number-one topic around the country, banks will be forced to open stock market booths with 'experts' giving out advice. Because these newly minted experts will be paid from the brokerage arm of the bank, 'maximizing your returns' will surely involve numerous trades. With the click of a button, your funds will gradually move from the cocoon and safety of the fixed-income arena into the playing field. Later, as the bull market pushes substantially higher, money earmarked as 'untouchable' will find its way into the riskiest areas of the stock market" (*Chapman Marketline*, 1987). Another mega bull warning signal will be banks vying with one another to handle the public's "portfolio."

When the home equity evolution began in the early 1980s, it was and continues to be a concern that at some point home equity, a sum based on the value of one's home, will find its way into the stock market. Low interest rates would encourage stocks to be bought on margin, or even on credit cards, as a "supercharged Dow" makes it impossible to resist a "sure thing." Eventually, as the stock market pushes into the stratosphere, bread-and-butter money is going to find its way into stocks and options—from bricks to paper.

When essential living-expense money is lost, it is vastly different to money lost in an "event." The reason why the 1987 crash was essentially just an "electronic event" was that the bulk of the money lost involved long-term investments. Time could heal that one. In October of 1929, it was the rent and daily-food money that was lost. Within days people were selling their cars to pay living expenses.

FROM COMPLACENCY TO EXCESSIVITY: CONSUMERISM AND ADVERTISING

In the mega bull market, advertising will infiltrate virtually every pore. Nothing will be sacred, not National Public Radio, public television stations, or the U.S. Postal Service—the last sacred cows of noncommercialism. The pervasiveness of commercialism will have infiltrated even the public school system as the final decade of the 1900s concluded the most extravagant spending spree of the century. Capitalism would be taken to its very extreme as country after country opened its arms to the concept of free enterprise, selling off every tangible asset they had. Everything would be for sale. Everything would have a price.

ADVERTISEMENTS PARALLELING THE HEIGHT OF THE STOCK MARKET IN THE FINAL PHASE

What happens over the coming few years should mirror well the emotions and values of the country as they change dramatically. In the next and final up phase of this mega bull market, the atmosphere will be charged with excitement. We will accept as normal the glorification of making money, as stocks make people wealthy beyond their wildest dreams. There will be advertising everywhere: covering buses and cars; huge flat-screen monitors that allow ads to be changed every few minutes; 60-foot holographic people, hands, animals, whatever—always selling, selling, selling. Supermarkets are already experimenting with smells to entice shoppers to various sections and aisles. We are becoming so immune to the pervasiveness of commercials that the commercial-free charter of National Public Radio and Public Television is really a metaphor for false advertising.

Wherever we go, even in countries around the world, the one common denominator constantly discussed will be the stock market. And stocks represent products. Long-term investments will become shorter and shorter trades.

ONCE IN PLACE A TREND ONLY STOPS WHEN ITS ORIGINAL INTENT IS FORGOTTEN

For the majority of investors, *the stock market has traditionally been an adjunct to their regular income.* Thought of as another way of building some security after retirement or in old age, the stock market usually functioned as a complementary way of enhancing one's Social Security or other retirement income. Dividends from utility or bond-type fixed-income financial instruments were the traditional source, which gave rise to the expression "good for widows and orphans" when talking of steady income investments. (Sounds so old fashioned today.) And, if there was perhaps some capital appreciation, it was a bonus, not an expectation. Now, a few minutes of waiting for capital gains feels like a lifetime. However, soon it will become a form of "salaried" game as thousands of investors give up their jobs to become "traders." The idea of playing the market is even being promulgated in schools, from elementary to college. It's possible that high schoolers and college students will give up their studies to become day traders. Slowly, investing will become a fad, and then a frenzy.

THE STOCK MARKET AS A GAME

With the use of computers growing exponentially in the last decade, it became obvious that the computer would allow easy accessibility to brokers. As the market went to new record levels, the public, trading more frequently, would push the volume of the New York Stock Exchange (NYSE) toward a one-billion-share day. "When the Nikkei finally succumbs, the void will be filled by the NYSE as one-billion-share days become average!" (*Chapman Marketline*, 1989). Now that trend is accelerating as Internet trading grows exponentially. (Even the conservative DJIA has been pressured into doing something righteously avoided up until now, succumbing to the pressure of having futures and options traded on a new DJIA Index.)

Eventually, 24-hour-a-day trading will become a magnet for money. With stock charts, unlimited market-related news and services, and the equivalent of the "No money down" operators of yore becoming stock seers, it will turn into a private game, played in pajamas, at home. The formality of traditional trading will be peeled away. When that final stock market bell silently rings one day, no one will understand whey the "market" opens limit down for days on end because "speculators" (as they were called in the stock pools of the twenties) will simultaneously be pushing the sell buttons on millions of computers around the world. And unfortunately, those sell orders will be answered by the longest busy signal in history. Their feelings will be similar to what those wealthy hol-iday makers aboard the "ocean liners to nowhere" in October of 1929 experienced as they watched glass-domed tickers spewing out unbelievably lower prices on their falling stocks. The only problem was, "modern" ticker or not, those prices were days late!

Another feature that appears at major stock market tops is the building of a new stock exchange venue offering the "biggest and best" state-of-the-art trading floor and data transmission. Unfortunately, no matter how big or modern the system (remember 1987?), it will fail when most needed.

CAPITALISM GOING AWRY

Capitalism is the current fashion/trend throughout the world, and the United States is essentially the creator of capitalism as we know it. When eventually our stock market becomes the most desirous place to invest, double-digit gains in the blue chips should become commonplace. As the DJIA powers relatively soon into the 10,000 (five-digit) level, other forms of investments should pale in comparison to the easy money that Wall Street will be dishing out. Intraday traders will probably see swings so large that entire fortunes will be made and lost in one session.

"NEW" PARADIGMS

By the time a "new" paradigm has been recognized by a majority of investors, it is closer to the end than the beginning. "Like a super-tanker slowing rounding a bend, the economy's positive turn won't be noticed until long after the smoke is left on the horizon" (*Chapman Marketline*, Summer 1986). It is time to look past the millennium.

While remaining a mega bull on the stock market (with a DJIA target of 22,000-plus by the summer of 2001), it is as important to recognize the signs of an approaching top now as it was at the 1982 bottom. After all, climbing the mountain is only one step; surviving the descent is equally as important.

If this stock market surge continues through the year 2000, and if the political and socioeconomic trends that perfectly match the 1920s template continue (as they should), then now is the time to start thinking about the consequences. It is a time to ruminate and circumscribe: Are we looking at another depression? Who will bail us out when there is no money left? Since a major top will almost certainly engulf the global community, if history is our guide, the answer is clear: *No one.* This is not necessarily a gloom-and-doom ultimate scenario, but rather an attempt to see where the logical conclusion and consequence lead us.

The questions continue. What happens if a cataclysmic scenario unfolds? How will the formerly communist and socialist societies cope when they have literally thrown out their secular ideology and core beliefs for capitalism? What if the rug suddenly gets pulled from under them? Where do they turn? Will there be a support system left at this rate (especially as almost every country is selling the infrastructure of their government property and services to the newly glorified free market system)? Are the disenfranchised to become the new rulers? And foremost, what will happen to our youth, many of whom have started life with nothing but luxury carriages and leather seats under their pampered bottoms? How will they deal with adversity? The generation that still shuts off the lights when leaving a room is almost gone. This is now an era of "forever golden."

SO WHAT DO I DO?

An orchestra conductor, in the middle of a piece, stops the orchestra. "No, no, no!" he says, waving his arms. "That's not how Beethoven wanted it. This is where Beethoven is strolling in the forest contemplating the melody of the slow movement. It's a beautiful late afternoon as the sunset filters through the leaves. Birds are in the trees, and–" Suddenly, he is interrupted by a trumpet player who asks impatiently, "Do I play louder or softer?" Just so, inpatient investors fume, "Forget the talk! Do I buy, or do I sell?!"

If the socioeconomic assumptions made are correct, implying that the next major up phase of the Dow Jones Industrial Average in this mega bull move is to the five-digit level, then the answer is easy. As long as one is invested in blue chip stocks or a growth-and-income fund that has a proven track record or the late cyclical stocks, just sit back and enjoy the ride. A reasonable strategy regarding preservation of capital–again, if this very long term prognosis is correct–should be to lighten up one's portfolio by a certain percentage as the DJIA goes parabolically higher.

THE DIFFICULTY WILL BE TO STEP OFF THE ACCELERATING TRAIN AT THE RIGHT STATION

Extricating oneself from a fully invested position is going to be an almost impossible task. Very few have the temperament of the famous investor Bernard Baruch, who sold his stocks before the 1929 crash. Selling when everyone is buying will be an extremely difficult task. The social pressure to be fully invested will be immense. Included in the list of enticements to get one into the stock market will be stock tickers at the bottom of virtually every news show on TV or on the Internet. Commissions on stocks should remain very low because high trading will eventually make the brokers money. Worse, your family, friends, and neighbors will constantly remind you how much they have made in "just a few days" (never mentioning how much they might have lost in "just a few days"). Anyone who lightened up on stocks in the summers of 1987 or 1997 can tell you how many times they were almost sucked back in, especially as they watched those big-point moves as the blue-chip stocks were hitting all-time highs.

When finally those icons discussed in the opening paragraph appear, time will be running out. No one knows the precise high or the time of the exact top, but this is a market that is essentially concluding about a century's worth of growth. If that assumption is correct, then, like the Nikkei before it, this bull market could go on for a great deal longer. It could also power very much higher than the targets set forth. Regardless, a strategy for exiting is as important as entering. We all know when to buy, but selling is a different story.

The forming of a major stock market top should be easily identifiable. However, amongst the plethora of "mega" everythings that are announced, yet another new building isn't going to stand out as anything very special. The project will have to be something really unusual to challenge a magnificent edifice such as the new Malaysian Petronas Towers. The person to build it will no doubt represent this age perfectly: a "self-made" entrepreneur easily recognizable by name in and out of his or her field, extremely rich, known for big mistakes and great comebacks, and who has a specific sense of style and a grandiose plan that somehow mixes personal ego with the entire country's exuberance.

IN CONCLUSION . . .

This chapter has attempted to deal with how history has repeated itself often enough in the stock market that some repetitive overlay can be used as a guidepost. While there are many technical and fundamental tools available to project numbers to the upside, it is the socioeconomic template that remains the key to this market's magnitude.

A mega bull market like this implies a once-in-a-generation opportunity. At this point, even another massive sell-off would only strengthen the longer-term prospects for this market. There is even a chance that instead of going to a top of major consequence early in the next decade, something of even a greater dynamic is happening. Perhaps, instead of making a final peak early in the next decade, this mega bull will just power higher and higher for another 10 years or longer, possibly even challenging the 30,000s as the Nikkei did. However, for now, the target of 22,000-plus by the summer of the year 2001 remains the target. Caveat emptor.

Only when the tulips fade, will the shine return to gold . . .

INDEX

Abnormal stock return (ABR), 107
Advertising, 185
Advisors
  criteria for changing, 157
  inexperienced, 168–169
Affiliation, with investments, 41–43, 70–71
Analysts
  accuracy of estimates made by, 2–4
  forecasts of, prolonged adjustment to new information, 142
  relationships to stocks, 71
  results of major errors by, 4–9
Anchoring, 70
Anxiety
  in bear markets, 65–66
  risk and, 19–20
Asian markets, 174
Attitudes, in organizational diagnosis, 96–97
Authority, 75–76

Banks, as contrary indicators for market, 183–184
Baring Brothers, 81
Baruch, Bernard, 164–165, 189
Beardstown Ladies, 168
Bear markets. *See also* Market fluctuations
  fear in, 65–66

Berkshire Hathaway, 66–67
Bernstein, Peter, 14
Bias, against selling, 35, 37–38
Book-to-market, price and earnings momentum and, 137–140
Brokers
  advice to buy versus sell from, 32–33
  cold calls from, responses to, 68–69
  compensation of, 81
  shifts in priorities and culture and, 80–82
Buffett, Warren, 62, 66, 71, 72, 75, 81, 161, 163, 164
Bull markets. *See also* Market fluctuations
  grandiosity and greed and, 24–25, 65
  sustainability of, 179–180
Buying, 43–44
  bias in favor of, 35, 37–38
  insider, 57
  optimism and, 31

Cabot Market Letter, 151
Cialdini, Robert, 60
Closure, brought by selling, 43–44
Cognitive dissonance, selling and, 39–43
Cold hands, 150–151